25 Tips for Productivity

Augusto Pinaud

Copyright © 2012 Augusto Pinaud

All rights reserved.

ISBN:1479311154
ISBN-13:978-1479311156

Cover Design by: Kenn Rudolph Design

http://kennrudolph.com

Copyright © Augusto Pinaud, 2012

All rights reserved. This book or any portion of it may not be reproduced or used in any manner without the express written permission of the publisher except for the use of brief quotations in book reviews or mentions of the book.

A mi mama… Quien puso en mis manos el primer libro en este tema e insistió que debía entenderlo, aun cuando no tenia la madurez necesaria.

To my mom… Who put in my hands my first book on this topic and insisted that I should understand it, even when I wasn't mature enough.

OTHER BOOKS BY THE AUTHOR

Fiction:
- The Writer
- Putsch. A Hannah Fisher Triller

Available on Amazon on PaperBack and Kindle.

CONTENTS

Dedication
Foreword by Tara Rodden Robinson - The Productivity Maven — Pg # 1
Introduction — Pg # 4
25: Do not do list — Pg # 9
24: Do not need list — Pg # 15
23: If you have cash flow, pay for those things that you don't enjoy and are cheaper than do it yourself — Pg # 20
22: Common Sense is uncommon — Pg # 25
21: Learn to type — Pg # 30
20: Automate Backups — Pg # 35
19: Don't ever use software that doesn't allow you to export your data — Pg # 40
18: If it doesn't work, get rid of it — Pg # 45
17: Don't be afraid of the short lived contexts — Pg # 50
16: Don't be afraid of the daily to do list — Pg # 54
15: Create a portable thinking environment — Pg # 58
14: Have more that one of the things you constantly use — Pg # 63
13: The reflection list — Pg # 68
12: Don't play with your productivity tools — Pg # 73
11: Get a Chair. A Good one I mean — Pg # 77
10: Plan the simple things — Pg # 81
9: Always carry your reading material — Pg # 85

8: Reduce our daily load	Pg # 88
7: Write down the key information - the key lists	Pg # 91
6: The Two browsers	Pg # 96
5: Discover your warning signs	Pg # 101
4: Plan for productive and focus time	Pg # 106
3: Giving yourself time after a trip to catch up	Pg # 111
2: Define your destination. On writing and in Detail	Pg # 116
1: Extraordinary Hour	Pg # 121
Conclusions and last notes	Pg # 126
Special Thanks	Pg # 129
About the Author	Pg # 130

FOREWORD

I met Augusto when he joined one of the first meetings of the GTD® Virtual Study Group, a twice monthly meeting of productivity enthusiasts that I host. How was I to know that enjoying his Venezuelan accent and warm humor would become such a familiar experience? What could have told me that we'd become such close friends--that I'd come to think of him as practically a brother? Was there any hint at how thoughtful, intelligent, and savvy he was? Well, yes. That part was clear from the beginning.

Now, all these years later, much has changed in my friend's life. He's become a father. He left sales and is now an accomplished novelist. He moved halfway across the country from L.A. to Ft. Wayne. What hasn't changed is our incredible friendship which has sustained me from afar, more times than I can count. When Augusto asked me to write this foreword, of course I said 'yes.' How could I say anything else? I have been the beneficiary of his guidance for years and years. Besides, to get an advance copy of his first work of non-fiction, his very first book on productivity? That was too good to pass up.

What you have in Augusto's 25 Tips is more than just a book of productivity hacks. What you have here is accumulated wisdom. Augusto has a real knack for seeing the inside of things and sharing perspective that can be life altering. I learned so much from this book and his tips gave me new insight into skills that I thought I knew well and practices I thought I'd perfected. I believe you'll find the same to be true.

There are so many great ideas here that when applied, will make a big difference. Whether it's acquiring or improving skills (like typing), making a daily to-do list, or looking beyond the obvious "common sense," you'll find a wealth of helpful advice, all delivered with Augusto's trademark humor and warmth.

Because of his schedule these days, whenever Augusto joins the Virtual Study Group meetings, it's a bit of an event. I always get a kick out of how much a celeb he's become to our listeners. It's all much deserved and well earned. I'm just grateful to be a part of his fan club. After you've read 25 Tips, you'll be a member of that club, too, I'm sure.

Tara Rodden Robinson
The Productivity Maven
August 2012.

INTRODUCTION

It wasn't until recently that I made peace with the fact that I am passionate about the topic of productivity, as passionate as I am about writing fiction. It was even more recently (after the first draft of this book was done) that Mike Vardy coined the term "productivityist" as an enthusiast of productivity and I was finally, accurately identified. I am no guru, nor an expert. I am simply a person who has enthusiastically experimented with productivity to ensure that the important and relevant stuff gets done. With that attitude in mind, I wrote this manuscript(even when I didn't consciously understand the concept that I was expressing).

The first book that I remember having read about anything related to productivity was The 7 Habits of Highly Effective People by Stephen R. Covey. I remember how much fun I made of my mother, who made her best effort to instill some of the principles in me, but in the immaturity of the moment I couldn't understand their importance.

Years have passed since those days and I have read many books since then. The writing in these pages has come from the ideas I have gleaned from many authors; maybe a combination of those is what made me compile these 25 ideas. Some have come from my enthusiasm for being more productive, others I have discovered by mistake.

For many years, like many people, I though that you could solve productivity issues just by finding the right tool and those tools taught me some of these tricks. But in reality, the tools by themselves are useless. Outlook, OmniFocus, Nozbe, the calendar or the to-do list are useless unless you understand first, their function and then, the reason for which you are using them and finally, what the tool itself brings to the table. It's not a secret that today my system lives in OmniFocus and as I write these lines, my productivity and systems are contained in an iPhone. But what allows me to be effective using the iPhone isn't OmniFocus. Years ago when my system was housed in Outlook, since my main machine was a PC with a Microsoft System

(I think I running Vista, maybe Windows 7) I wasn't effective because I was on a PC (please add your own joke here) or because I used Outlook (second chance to introduce your own joke). I was effective because I had discovered some of these tricks and it was the tricks, not the tools I used, that allowed me to do the things I did.

In my journey of productivity I have made many good calls and even more mistakes. Maybe that is the reason that when something works, I don't try to change it; that is, I don't try to change it until it stops working. I'm not tempted to try out new systems, either. Not because I don't think they might be better options, but because the one I'm using works incredibly well. I prefer to use my energy on more productive stuff. I don't use an iPhone because I believe that Apple products are free of problems and limitations (they have both, more than people believe). Instead, I use them because while they don't do everything, what they do, they do incredibly well and without any effort on my part (and that last part is the key).

When I first started out, I used a Palm Pilot, beginning with the the Personal, and updated constantly until the Treo 680. I was able to do things with a Palm that most people consider impossible: reading books, changing calendars when Palm introduced categories and colors (which, in my model, "supposedly" were not compatible), I installed applications, and more. I invested uncountable hours so that the tool would do what I wanted it to do, and in many cases it was a productivity tool and maybe more for distraction and play.

I don't know how many hours I've spent restoring operating systems. However, one day I finally understood that I could be using that time to accomplish other objectives, and since I realized that I could use the time in a better way,, that is one of my objectives.

I have learned not to hunt solutions to problems I don't have, but instead how to reduce, improve, and eliminate those that are real. For example, my iPhone doesn't allow me to place a clock on the background screen but that is not a real problem: I can see the time at the top of the screen or wear a watch. Therefore, I haven't invested a second trying to fix this "problem," a thing that without a doubt I would have done in my years on the Palm.

If you browse the Table of Contents, you may have noticed that the chapters go from 25 to 1 instead of 1 to 25. The reason for that isn't to give any of these tricks more importance than any other, but instead reflects how important a personal impact that these things have had in my life and in the results I had obtained. These are the tricks I have learned, that I use and that help me to be a better person, boss, father, husband, and friend.

The reason why I talk about productivity is that it is one of those things I need constantly. My tendency to get distracted requires that I use many tricks to keep me oriented towards my objectives. Or as my wife puts it, my ability to get distracted and waste time is almost unlimited. That is the reason I have learned these tricks that allow me to maintain my attention (or more likely allow me to reduce the effects of my distractibility) and it is these 25 tricks that I compile here.

If you discover something here that works for you and helps you, I have achieved my goal. If you know of someone that can benefit from this, share the trick or better yet, give them a copy of the book.

Again, many of these tricks aren't original to me, I didn't invent them, and some of them I can't remember where I saw them for the first time. If I omit giving credit to the correct person, I apologize in advance, that wasn't my intention. But if that has happened, let me know so I can correct it in future editions of this book.

Without further ado, thanks for reading these tricks and I hope you find some that will be useful.

25: DO NOT DO LIST

The first time I heard about keeping a Do Not Do List was in a post on Michael Hyatt's blog. Back then he was still the CEO of Thomas Nelson (he's since retired), and he mentioned the things he needed to be reminded to stop doing. Immediately, I began my own DO NOT DO LIST.

My list has had many versions, but I think none of the original items have disappeared, simply more things have been added. These are things that without a doubt, I need to be constantly reminded that are not worthy of my time or effort.

The idea of the list is simple: Remind me of what I should stop doing or better yet, won't ever do. For example, the list contains things that I should delegate or hire someone else to do. Even when I can do these tasks myself, others can do a better job than I can and much faster than I, allowing me to spend my time on more important stuff. This last element is the key.

Washing a car, for example, usually costs less than US$20. If I do it myself, it will take at least half an hour. Assuming that I can earn than $20 in half an hour, it makes more sense to hire someone else to do the job so I am free to earn income. In other words, I estimate the dollar value of my time and use that as one way of deciding what "not to do." Remember, this is a private list that no one else needs to see. You don't need to justify your list to anybody. To give you some ideas about creating your own list, here are a few of the items I keep on my own Do Not Do List:

- Don't wash the car myself.

I know some people love washing their own cars, and are content to spend hours on the job, lovingly soaping, rinsing, drying and even waxing. Not me. I not only I don't enjoy washing my car, it leaves me in a terrible mood and feels like a total waste of time and energy. Factoring in the cost and what my time is worth, it was a no-brainer to add this to my Do Not Do List. The reason it is in the top, was only because it was the first item that I thought of when I created the list.

- Don't finish a book if, after I've read twenty-five percent, it's either not good or I am not interested.

I love to read, and when I was little, my mom used to tell me that I was like a library rat that always needed to be around books. The problem is that not all books deserve to be finished. (This includes, for some readers, even if it hurts, those that I have written.) The relationship between a reader and a book is personal. There are books that make us dream and that make us cry; those same books, in the hands of other people, will not only not produce those effects, but actually the opposite.

It took me years to give myself permission to not finish a book. It wasn't until I read Steve Leveen's The Little Guide to Your Well Read Life that I was introduced to the idea that it was okay to abandon a book after 50 pages. Normally, I try to read more than that, but on occasion fifty pages is more than enough.

- Don't store critical information on mobile devices if the software doesn't allow backup.

The reason is simple: I have learned that technology can fail. (For many people, it is only other people's technology that can fail... until theirs fails.) When information stored on mobile apps can't be backed up, and when a failure occurs, all the content will disappear, but even worse, it may disappear forever.

My first electronic organizer was a Casio. I have fond memories of that Casio, until the day I lost everything on it. After trying to recover my data, I had a tantrum, and considered the consequences my setup. That's the reason I chose to switch to the Palm Pilot: not only could I do a backup, but it was easy to do. Sadly, my legendary Casio crash wasn't the only time I lost my data, but it was many years later and not quite as painful as that first time. It isn't enough to have backup systems, if you don't use them. It sounds obvious, but many people simply don't backup their info, even when the system exists to allow them to do so.

- Don't test new systems or play with tools on computers that I use make a living.

This was one of the costly and painful lessons I've learned. As I said in the introduction of this book: "I don't know how many hours I've spent restoring operating systems. However,one day I finally understood that I could be using that time to accomplish other objectives, and since then, that is one of my objectives."

As a nerd, I understand electronics and computers and I love a "Beta." I am attracted to software that the public hasn't used, and that isn't on the market yet. Before I added this item to my Do Not Do list, my work computer was running Vista, when it was still in Beta. On a Friday afternoon, at about 6 PM, I was playing with something new and my laptop crashed. The following Monday, I was supposed to fly from Los Angeles to Miami to attend a meeting that had taken months to set up. It took me fourteen hours of trying before I was forced to admit defeat and buy another laptop. My presentation was gone and I had to rebuild it over the weekend.

Now, my main work machine is sacred, and I have a second one for playing, testing, and having adventures, one that is pretty much disposable. It was a painful way to learn that when I want to play, play somewhere else, far away from the tools I need to make my living.

- Don't eat my frustrations.

This one is a little more personal. At the time of this writing, I weigh 120 pounds less than when I created this rule. Obviously it wasn't only this Do Not Do that made me lose the weight, but it's helped me avoid overeating when I am frustrated or angry as I would have done in the past. When the need is too great, I have learned that I can drink all the water that I want, but I don't allow myself to eat until the frustration or the reason I was angry is gone. I have failed a lot on this, but it is much better and continues to get better. This is perhaps one of the most important rules for my health.

These are not all the items on my Do Not Do list, but I hope these are enough to explain the principle and get some ideas for what you might put on your own. Many times it is harder to say 'no' to the things that you know are easy to do, in just a couple of minutes time(this is one of the most common lies that we tell to ourselves), because it seems as if getting someone else to do it would be a waste of money and time (and that's not always true).

24: DO NOT NEED LIST

This is a much more recent item in my arsenal of tricks. When I began reading about minimalism, I started to understand that a more minimalist lifestyle was a good complement for productivity. By having less stuff, I spend less time maintaining and taking care of stuff. This means I have more time to enjoy the activities that I like and that call my attention. However, people practicing minimalism often aim to levels of reduction that far exceed what I'm comfortable with. Like Colin Wright who lives with only 51 items, or Tammy Strobel and her 72 things or Nina Yau who claims to need only 47 possessions. Without a doubt, there are things that I want to have and many more that I want to enjoy, and that number surpasses Tammy Strobel's 72 possessions (and honestly, by a lot).

Without aiming for extremes, I am attracted to the idea of reducing the number of my possessions, especially to eliminate all those things that I don't use, that don't work, or whose only purpose is to take up space. I want my possessions to be useful stuff. Essayist Patrick Rhone doesn't speak of minimalism, but instead about 'enough.' It was when I discovered Patrick's writing that I recognized what it was I was looking for. I want what I need, but not the excess. When I tried to understand what having enough means to me, I began to consider those things that I don't need, that even when they call my attention and I'm able to buy them, they aren't going to improve my life. Once I understood what I really wanted, I felt much more freedom of let go all those things that I'm not using .

The a perfect example of a "Do Not Need" item on my list is the 27 inch Apple monitor. It is simply beautiful and each time that I see it, I imagine how beautiful will look on my desk (ok, maybe on the desk I dream of having, since the one I have is a temporary one that I've had for the last five years or so). When I think about owning this Apple monitor, I imagine the incredible feeling I'd have when I was working on it, and all that I would be able to do see on that huge expanse. But honestly I don't need it, and in the end, I think it would be a cause for distraction. A monitor that big, without a doubt, would allow me to get distracted without me noticing it how distracted I am. I have learned that my monitors need to be small, because it's hard to see more than one application at the time.

I have an incredible weakness for suitcases, bags, backpacks, books, pens, electronics, accessories of all kinds, and more. The Do Not Need List contains more than fifty items. From clothes to electronics everything in between including a convertible that I've dreamed about for years. Once in a while, I consider that car again, but in my notes is the reason why don't need a convertible, including that I had one and didn't enjoy it as much as I thought I was going to. I was uncomfortable in it when was too hot and uncomfortable in it when was too cold. Also, I didn't like being that close to the ground. As part of that same explanation, I remind myself how much I enjoyed my Jeep Wrangler, so if I ever do need a convertible, that should be the model.

The objective of the Do Not Need list, is to help me to reach that place of having enough. It is not that I can;t use one more shirt, or one more pair of shoes or a pen or a new notebook. Is simply that I don't need it; I have all the shirts I need, and the shoes that use and are comfortable (the most important prerequisite for a shoe in my opinion: they need to be comfortable). I have a pen that I love how it writes and white paper on which to write my ideas. I don't need more than one pen, nor do I want a different notebook, in this department I have enough. (Yes, Pens are on the list.)

As I said before, my objective isn't to be a minimalist, but to have enough, and even if that is a state that changes and evolves, I understand that when I have fewer possessions my attention is less fragmented and the higher chance I have to make something useful, which is, at the end of the day, the reason why I want to be more productive. Many of the items on my Do Not Need list are things I think about constantly, and are things that I would love to have, just to have them. That is because in some part of my mind, I've convinced myself that these will do me good, make my life easier or help me to enjoy something much more. But when I considered it more deeply, I understood that the item is not something I really need and that many of these are whims from a time in which I believed that things (especially an abundance of them) were going to make me happy.

Here are a few of the items on my Do Not Need list:

- 27 inch Apple monitor
- iPhone 4S (My iPhone 4 is perfectly serviceable)
- iPad2 (if I get a new one, it will be a newer model)
- Cheap t-Shirts
- New TV for the house
- The printed versions of my books

Today, these are the things are on my list because in this moment I only need to have enough and I understand that none of these will make me happier or a better person. Having these things may disrupt the equilibrium that I am trying to create, that of having enough.

23: IF YOU HAVE CASH FLOW, PAY FOR SOMEONE ELSE TO DO THOSE THINGS THAT YOU DON'T ENJOY DOING AND ARE CHEAPER THAN DOING THEM YOURSELF

The key phrase is cash flow. Getting in debt while you escape from doing the stuff that you don't enjoy will simply generate more things that you will not enjoy in the long term (or at least things that I didn't enjoy in the long term).

How much do you make per hour? Let's make the following

calculations; if you make $40,000 per year, that means that you make $769 per week (more or less). Assuming that you work 40 hours a week, that means that you make roughly $19 per hour. If you can, use that hour productively instead of spending it doing things you don't enjoy and that don't generate income. At first glance, it seems like there are only a few things you can hire out, but you won't believe how many other possibilities exist--many more than what you imagine because the hours accumulate faster than you would expect.

For example, if you hate mowing and caring for the lawn, but you enjoy spending time outside, hire someone to take care of it for you. Again, assuming that you have the cash flow, determine how much your time is worth and search for a more effective service. If someone were to pay me to wash a car, it would cost around $50 for a mediocre job, so it is always cheaper go to the automatic car wash and for much less cost, get a clean car (also the car wash always does a better and cheaper job).

Once you start making a list of these things, you'll be amazed how many things can go on it: wash the car, mow the lawn, clean the house, maintain computers, install a professional sound system, paint the house, install lamps, install floors, or decorate the house. At the same time, make a list of what are you going to do with the time that you are going to free up, like read, play with the kids, walk the dog, meditate or do yoga, among others.

The possibilities are endless and the time that you can free is equally endless. I know people who enjoy mowing the lawn, washing the car, cleaning the house, and polishing the copper. Just because other people enjoy these activities doesn't mean that you have to or that you should feel guilty because you don't enjoy them. This last part is one of the biggest secrets. My neighbor mows his lawn twice a week with a big smile in his face. I haven't mowed my own lawn in two years and don't plan to do it any time soon. My wife is an incredible cook, and homecooked is the best food we can eat. For others, making a grilled sandwich is almost considered a punishment. The problem isn't in the things you enjoy, but in those that you have to do and don't enjoy; on those, decide which ones you can pay someone else to do and use that time for something useful or that you enjoy. Pay someone to clean the house and go to the gym instead.

The problem is never the time that the activity takes, that's where most people make the mistake, in thinking something like, "But washing the car takes just half an hour." That may be true, but if it takes you another thirty minutes to lose the feeling of frustration produced by doing the activity, then it cost you an hour. If there is any doubt, washing my car is one of those things that I try my best to never do, no matter what. I take the car to the car wash and read a book during the fifteen or twenty minutes that it takes them wash it. My time reading is more than worth more than the cost of car wash, including the tip.

25 TIPS FOR PRODUCTIVITY

The objective of this exercise is productivity, and to be productive we need to stop doing those things which waste our abilities. Productivity is not doing more things, but doing the right things, the things that are going to help us to move forward. The things that will create an effect immediately or in the future generate more or greater satisfaction. It isn't that we can't do three things at the same time, is that if we focus in doing each thing with all our attention, we will spend half of the time.

Personally, I have a passion for anything related to fixing computers. In general, though, it's not cost effective for me to spend my own time fixing my computers. On the other hand, it's something that makes me feel good and that I enjoy, it keeps me entertained. For that reason, I am willing to repair, clean, and update computers of many friends and family. I do this even when the cost per hour, in most cases, makes it cheaper to send them to the technician. But in this case, it's something that I honestly enjoy. I can spend hours on it and reach that mysterious place that Mihaly Csikszentmihalyi mentions in his book Flow, where time seems to stand still. I enjoy repairing computers so much that even when it take me an hour or two, I end up feeling full of energy and satisfied. (That is, in general, a sign that something that can be consider productive: if it leaves you feeling full of energy.)

I've mentioned how much I dislike washing my car. Even if it only take ten minutes, it leaves me in a bad mood, without energy, and then I need to recover; and it's something that I do only with resignation. If I have enough cash flow, I always pay for things like this that I don't enjoy.

Remember that wasting two hours (one working, one recovering) doing something that someone else can do better at a lower cost than you can is exactly the opposite of efficiency and productivity. If you dislike washing clothes, for example, find a service and then use that time for something productive like reading, playing with your kids, cooking a special dish, sitting on the patio or in the backyard to breathe or simply rest. Many times rest is the most productive thing that we can do and, in general, it's at the bottom of the list when we consider productive things.

22: COMMON SENSE IS UNCOMMON

Who called common sense, common? I've discovered that what people call "common sense" is, in reality, not common. If you look a the definition of "common," you'll find that refers to something ordinary, frequent accepted as normal by the majority. This last part is exactly what makes it common: "accepted as normal by the majority." The problem is that "common sense" isn't something shared by the majority of people. In fact, it is a concept that escapes the large majority of people except in those things where they are experts (or at least skilled). In those cases, it seems like "common sense" because they assume that the knowledge they have is everyone should know. Sadly, there is nothing farther from reality. "Common sense" is simply something not common.

Consider something that it is common sense. For example, in an ice cream pasteurizer, there is a limit, a point at which the thickness (that is, the viscosity) of the ice cream will exceed the capacity of the machine. If the ice cream is too thick it will clog up the machine. That's common sense to the machine's operator and the engineer who designs the ice cream factory knows it, too. For them, this is common sense.

Imagine that you're going to repair your own car. Did you know that when you are going to work under your car, you shouldn't do it with the car up on jacks but instead by using supports? For someone who works on cars constantly, this is common sense (and a safety precaution). For the person who has never been under a car, it's not.

Is it common sense that when you are traveling by air, you're not going to be able to use your electronics except during certain parts of the flight? Not for everyone; for a lot of people that is not common knowledge, or logical, for them it is not common sense.

That's the problem with many of the tricks and methods for productivity. In my case, I am a medium-advanced user of Excel. This means that I can make macros and do some stuff that other people can't even dream about doing. For me to write a macro and solve some problems in Excel so that it does what I need it to is common sense. Not because it can't be done a different way, but simply because with the macro I can accomplish what I want up to ten times faster (or more). For me, implementing a macro is common sense; for the majority of Excel users, though, it's not even an option. (There are many people--more than what you might think--that don't know what a macro is, much less that Excel can do that.)

That's one of biggest problems when we consider common sense in productivity, since common sense is something not real, applying it to productivity is basically impossible. In the tech-rich nations, there is a boom in the culture of "hacking" things and principles, and many of these hacks are things that are common sense for some, a significant improvement for others and in some cases even life changing. When David Allen talks about the principles behind his book Getting Things Done, he says his method is just the application of the obvious. There are thousands of people flocking to Getting Things Done for help--but for Allen, his approach is self-evident--for him, it's merely common sense.

The point is that we all assume that common principles exist and are universal, and that only a few weird people lack this wrongly named "common sense." The reality is, that in general, unless we are teaching something to others, we assume that people have the same ability to understand and possess the same knowledge that we do, and that makes the knowledge public and general.

The interesting question from the productive point of view is what happens when we stop assuming the existence of so-called common sense. For example, if we receive an email that it is short and at the bottom is the signature, "Sent from my Phone," we consider that it's fine that it was short. But if we receive the same email, and it comes from somebody's laptop, many people get offended that the message is short and direct. Is it common sense that from the phone you are going to write emails that short and to the point?

You need another example of this wrongfully named common sense? Common sense says that if I have an inbox tray on my desk, and you are bringing something to my world, you are going to place the item in the inbox. How many times has your office's internal mail been dropped on your chair, or on your laptop? It would seem as if using the inbox would be obvious and common sense but not to the mail carrier.

The last example of common sense is in the messages that you are constantly sending, the form letters, those messages that you send repeatedly. For many productive people that I know, it is common sense that they write the message once, and then create an email signature out of it or save it to a so that they can simply copy and paste the text the next time they need it. For those people, this is common sense, and is also an effective, time-saving method . Sadly, many people lack this kind of common sense and every time they reply to that sort of message, they write it again from scratch. The idea of using it as a signature or copy and paste the text is simply foreign to them.

21: LEARN TO TYPE

This is one of those things that a lot of people ignore. When we talk about typing, many believe that two fingers is enough. These same people make excuses like, "I don't need to be faster than what I am." Or, I am incredibly fast with two fingers." I've made those and many other excuses. The reality is that the majority of us spend more hours in front of a keyboard that anywhere else, but we neglect working on improving our use of it and consider that it is ok to be mediocre at it.

The reasoning is simple, it's the mentality that improvement is going to be useful. But let's look at the following:

Imagine that on an average day, you write emails, responding to a friend's comments on Facebook, doing some searches in the browser, and you draft a short report: that's about 4,000 words in day. (Trust me, that's not a lot. Together, the first four chapters of this book were more 5,000 words.) We'll also assume that your average typing speed is 25 words per minute. (I'm sure you're faster than that, but if you were to get tested you would be surprised what your actual speed is.) That means that you need around 2.66 hours, or approximately two hours and fifty minutes to do your writing on that average day. And that's only keyboard typing. Let's assume that you take my advice and learn to be mediocre on the keyboard and reach 45 words per minute. That same 4,000 words now can be written in 1.48 hours or, more or less, one hour and fifty minutes. In case of any doubt, you just gained 50 minutes per day. Now imagine that you learn to type 100 words per minute, that means that you can do the same 4,000 words in 40 minutes, saving you two hours of your time. (This is the two hours of time that you are constantly looking for and wish you had.)

Imagine what you could do in two hours of extra time! At least, it might guarantee that you will be able to leave work by 5 PM and go home. The best part is that typing faster is it's easy to learn, it's free, and it lasts forever.

I resisted this idea for the longest time; I was really fast typing just with my two fingers, and I thought I didn't need more, until I discovered how much time I could gain. In that moment, I sat and learned. (I still consider myself mediocre as a typist and I continue practicing. My speed at the time of this writing is around 85 words per minute. My goal is to write over 100 words per minute before the end of 2012.)

When I got my first iPad was the first time I noticed the difference in typing speed on the screen versus an external keyboard. Even today, most of my writing is done using an external keyboard. But there are moments when I am interested in writing and I don't need to write quickly (like when I am journaling) but writing on the screen unbearably slow. Back then, I was tapping out words on the screen at roughly 18 words per minute. I began to look for solutions for an external keyboard that was more permanent, but I wasn't willing to go to a keyboard that wasn't full size, honestly, I can't stand small keyboards.. I was in that hunting process when my friend Andre Kibbe asked me why I wasn't searching for software to teach me how to type quickly using the screen. (If you read the previous chapter, this is another example of "common sense.") Why this had not crossed my mind, I have no idea, but immediately I found an app and began practicing. I'm still really slow, but am able to type around 60 words per minute now. For a lot of people, that's a speed that they don't believe is possible to attain. I want to get faster; I've heard there are people typing on the iPad screen at more than 90 words per minute and I don't see why I can't accomplish that. Maybe some day, I won't need the external keyboard at all anymore.

If you had read until here, this is going to be in my opinion the chapter of this book that it is going to be the least read. Many people that are really fast using two fingers don't need typing, because not only they are really fast but also they don't type anything long enough to make learning to type worth the effort.

If you've read this far and you still don't see the importance of learning how to type well, or think this is not something that you should learn right now consider the following: A bottleneck is a phenomenon where the capacity and the performance of the whole system is affected by one element.

If you are like me and you work eight hours a day, of which you spend the half or your time typing, being slow is the most significant bottleneck in your productivity, even more than conference calls and meetings that you are sitting in only because you have to be there.

Assuming that in fact you type 25 words per minute, (I invite you to do a free test on the internet; the result can be more impressive than what you think) and I type 85 words per minute, you will need 39 minutes to type 974 words and I will be ready in 11 minutes and 30 seconds. Now lets multiply the difference of 27 minutes five times (137 minutes or 2.3 hours.) That's the advantage that, in any day of the week, you can gain if you learn to type. In case you missed the other math part, that calculation was for one day, so you will be really getting more than 10 hours per week.

20: AUTOMATE BACKUPS

This is one of those things that was hard for me to learn in a certain time of my life... I am not sure that I learned or that Apple made it so easy with Time Capsule, but it is without a doubt something that I am grateful for.

The reality is that hard drives fail, get corrupted, and get lost. Many times, they contain all the photos from the last ten years or a whole collection of movies or the thesis or the book that you have been writing the last six months. In a second, without you understanding why or how, everything is gone. All that is left is tears of frustration and the thinking that you should have done the backup that you'd been avoiding for the last month.

In general we are running constantly, we have accepted more things to do than are humanly possible. And we have even more things waiting to see if we get the chance to do a couple more things! The only thing it seems we've forgotten is rest and to take time for those things that are important, like backing up key files. (For many people, these pertain to family and health.)

There are thousand of products on the market, for PC and Mac, that allow you to do your backups automatically and fast. The hours that potentially you can save not having to deal with this problem, is worth every minute that you are going to "waste" setting it up. Despite what you might think, all of us have the time to stop, buy a external hard drive, get and install the software, learn how it works, get a second back up for the backup. The issue, if you think about it, is do you have the time to rebuild everything? Imagine for a moment that your hard drive failed right now... what you will lose? Which file or files are going to make you spend the next hours hoping for a miracle? What do you need so you make that backup right now and get some mental peace?

As I wrote in other essays in this book, I love to be in front of the computer and I love to help people with their computer problems. I have created backup solutions semi-automated and fully-automated for many of my close friends. In my experience, all those backups that were semi-automatic, always end up failing; because the people never get into the habit of making the backup.

Books (many friends have lost their books that they had months working on), university theses, work for school, annual reports, business plans, marketing campaigns, Power Point presentations (especially half an hour before the time of the presentation: technology almost never fails when you have time to fix it and solve it), collections of music, movies and more; all those victims of the "this weekend I was going to make the backup" syndrome. In most of these cases, the losses are simply impossible to recover.

The problem is that we always think that it is the other person's computer is the one that will fail, especially when ours has failed already and there are a large number of electronics (many of which we don't consider computers, like the iPod, iPad, iPhone, Android Phone and more) and we don't think about what would happen if we lost that information. I feel so sad I hear things like this: "I lost all the contacts on my Blackberry, please send me the numbers and the pins" or when they say: "I lost my phone, can someone send me the numbers of my friends" and even more sad when you read things like: "Someone know how to save a hard drive, mine is making a terrible noise and doesn't start."

In all those cases, the problem begins because the lack of backup, in all those examples it would had been really simple to establish an automated backup system that would had saved the pain that these people are living (and that even more sadly, that many more people will suffer.)

I understand that not everyone has the technical knowledge to create the system for automated backups; for many people this is simply something that they don't know exists as a possibility, something that is practically in another language (one that they don't speak). But these are the people who suffer, regardless of what their backup method is. Find someone that can help you, pay someone to help you, hire a service: how you get the backup is irrelevant.

If you can't justify the initial cost, think for a moment of the cost if something failed. My collection of music is around 2,150 songs, 15.65GB. It's possible that I could purchase many of those songs again, but 2,150 songs... at $.99 cents per song... it isn't necessary to do the math ($2,128.50 plus tax). An automated system costs much less than that with the external hard drive, too. A DropBox account of 50GB (were you will get a lot of free space) costs around $100 per year, for the price of the music collection alone, it would take me 20 years to match the cost of a DropBox account. In the case of iCloud (the Apple Solution) for $40 per year, you get 25GB (and anything that you purchase from them doesn't count toward that limit) so in this solution it would take more than 53 years to match the cost of replacing my music collection. Like I said, from my point of view it seems really cheap; sadly, most people will lose a fortune when they lose everything or they simply resign and console themselves saying things like: "I lost all my music, but regardless, most of it I didn't like, so it's an opportunity to purge the trash." (Yes, someone told me that after they lost their music for lack of backup.)

When the crash happens is not the moment to feel sorry; once it happens, there is nothing you can do (in most cases). The question is: why you didn't make it automatic before it happened, before it was a problem? The interesting thing is that many people will not even start to make amends after it happens. They think, "You know, it happened already, it will not happen to me again." Maybe it's one of those things that we never consider, but that their effects are just devastating.

19: DON'T EVER USE SOFTWARE THAT DOESN'T ALLOW YOU TO EXPORT YOUR DATA

Do not ever use software that doesn't allow you to export your data. Let me repeat this, it is important. Do not ever use software that doesn't allow you to get your information out of it in a format that can be opened and used somewhere else. This is one of those interesting things that we do to ourselves. We begin using this great software that it is going to help us to do this or that, and it is going to change the way we do things, we are going to gain time, use it to have our journal in a secure and private manner, it is going to change our life and it is going to make us happy and when everything is there, the software simply... fails!

That's when we discover that the software doesn't allow for backup, and that all the information that you had entrusted to it is gone. I am sure that this has NEVER happened to YOU, but it has happened to ME.

Products that were going to change my life (ironically maybe they did, but in a different way), that were going to save me a lot of time, (but when they failed I wasted even more than the amount saved). Products that were going to generate incredible results--now they simply generate incredible frustration and an even bigger waste of time. Not only do I need to recover the information, but I have to invest hours searching, entering the information again into their software or the replacement. The most interesting part is, that in general, we continue to use the same software; this seems to be one of the hardest lessons to learn and when it fails again, we argue that it will not fail after that...

It is your right as a user to export your information, to move it (easily) from one place to another and to back up your data so it doesn't get lost. What happens is that when we see the shiny object, the one that gets our attention, the one that will change our life, we forget that we should check things as important and transcendent as the possibility of exporting.

Through the years I have learned the value of text files, not for anything else than the ease of switching platforms, with the ease that almost any software can open a text file, the ease that makes backing up and exporting into something super simple. Maybe it's important to clarify that for many applications that I use, the ability to backup and export doesn't necessarily have to be part of the application, but at least, the resulting files of the application need to be accessible from others. For example Microsoft Word, doesn't back up your files, but the resulting file is easy to export to other formats and even open in other applications. The same is true for iTunes. The problem is when the software doesn't allow you to export the information or save the content, or even migrate the content, because it is in their proprietary format.. (I tend to have problems with proprietary formats; you should be able to open files in more than one application. No one thinks that software will cease to exist, but it happens and today files created in that software can't be opened.) Sadly, there are applications for which generating an export is a Solomonic work and in many cases is impossible. Like I said before, in my opinion is my right as user to export my files, be able to move them (easily) from one place to another; but I also understand is the programer's right to build a software in the way he sees fit. But if it is not easy, obvious, and fast to export my data, I am not interested. Again, thanks a lot!

Imagine for a moment that your smart phone or tablet failed. What you will lose? What software doesn't have backups or doesn't allow you to export the information and because of that you have no backup? Not too long ago, my iPhone fell in the hands of my daughter. Twenty minutes later the smart phone was dead; it didn't work anymore. Without putting a finger on who was guilty (I was, for those who have any doubt about it) I got into my car, drove to the closest Apple Store, and bought a new phone. In the same store, I connected to the Mac, and I didn't leave the store until all my information was on my new phone: all my applications, games, music, and more importantly all my information was back. (Including the recipes in the software that my wife and I use, my journal notes, my notes about changing the world, my pending games and more.) In other words, my information was safely backed up and was really easy to restore to have my phone in full operative mode. If I choose to leave the apple iOS ecosystem tomorrow, every one of the applications that contain my information today allow me not only to export my data, but to easily access it in the new device, regardless of the operating system.

I would love to say that it has always been like that, but in reality hasn't. Many times I've lost all the information, all the phone numbers, all my notes, all the calendar appointments, or worse, I didn't lose anything but I had to enter it to manually. (In some cases, it would had been better to just lose the information; manually entering all the data is one of those things that I am sure can be used as punishment.) For many years, my backup was a printed copy of my calendar, all my contacts, my notes... Every Friday, I would print all the contacts, notes, and the next eight weeks of calendar. If something happened, I used to assume that eight weeks would had been enough to rebuild the future ones. Every time that the technology failed, (even when the failure was my fault) I had to begin from scratch, take all the pages, and type all the information. That happened more than I wish to remember, but taught me another trick (or lesson) that I will be talking about later in the book. (If you want to flip ahead, it's Chapter 12:Do not play with your tools of productivity - and income generators)

Today, if a software, application, or electronic tool doesn't allow me to export and backup my information, I am simply not interested in how fantastic the software, application or electronic tool might be, or the how my life is going to be changed. If they can't backup my information, it's nothing that I should use. I have saved myself many headaches with this trick.

I know it's hard to resist the shiny object, but remember that this object that is going to change your life, in which you are going to invest your time and your energy (and in many cases your heart) without the ability to backup, can like magic, make everything disappear... and doesn't matter the size, quantity, or the amount of tears. Those tears are not going to make your data show up again.

18: IF IT DOESN'T WORK, GET RID OF IT

When was the last time you spend $300, $500, $1000 on something that doesn't fulfill your purpose? Why, if you know that it is not going to be useful for your purpose, do you keep it? Ah! Because you spent a lot of money on it... I have also paid a lot of money for many things that were nothing more than technological trash.

Just because you paid a lot for something doesn't mean that it's going to be useful, or that will be useful later on. I am not saying don't buy anything expensive; what I'm trying to say, is that if what you buy doesn't work, or more specifically doesn't work for you, it should be removed from your world with the same emotion that you had when you bought it.

For me, this include many things: bags, suitcases, software, tables, shoes, pants, and many more.

In 2007, when my PC failed (one of those times that the hard drive failure happened to other people, because if you remember most people don't backup because hard drives and computers fail to others, but not to us), I went and bought a MacBook and declared war on the PC. The mistake wasn't in the purchase of the Mac, actually two years later I got another Mac (same model, newer generation). I spend the following Saturday and Sunday getting the new machine ready (and recreating the presentation that was lost when the hard drive failed; of course I didn't had a backup - at that time I wasn't doing what I talked about in the previous two chapters.) On the next Monday, I began the pilgrimage of my work trip. The problem was it hadn't occurred to me that my Treo 650 was going to be allergic to the Mac. I lost information in the process of syncing (fortunately, this information was backed up), but I wasted uncountable hours and got really mad (with myself). Twelve days later I was buying another PC. I had spent twelve days during which instead of being productive, I was trying to see how I was going to make something work that wasn't working for me. On the thirteenth day, I was working like I should. When say 'should,' it was because the needs of the moment were created around a PC, not around a Mac.

But I learned an important lesson. If my memory doesn't fail me, was on day twelve that I read a post from Eric Mack where he said exactly that: "If doesn't work get rid of it," and the next day I assembled the PC and got back all my productivity as I was used to.

The next mistake of this kind was less expensive. I got an Acer Aspire. The netbooks where hot, and sounded like a good solution. It was slow (even with the maximum of memory ram) but the major issue was one that even today I have not been able to let go of: the size of the keyboard. My typing speed was incredibly affected by the reduction in size of the keyboard. It wasn't the size of the screen so much as it was the fact that the keyboard was annoying. It just wasn't efficient. In a short time, the Acer was on the shelf and a little later in the hands of someone who was in need of a computer and didn't have one. In this case, I used some of the stuff I had learned with the 2007 Mac experiment. I carried the Acer with me for a while, and tried to use it, but since wasn't a practical machine, regardless of what I paid for it, it simply went to the shelf until I was able to put it in the hands of someone that would appreciate it.

Two years later I moved back to the Mac, but this time, before I got the Mac, I knew what to expect. By then I had my iPhone (first generation) and I was sure that the problems were going to be minor ones (even though some weren't) but this time I spend hours getting the plan ready, before the big move. After the change, I have never had the need to return to a PC. If I would need to, the first thing I would want to know would be how my workflow was going to be affected, that is even before I want to see what the market has that can interest me... The problem is not the cost of toy, the application, or the tool, but the hidden cost that is going to be created when everything else gets affected.

But the lesson that was really important and that I have applied to many products that I had gotten over the years with the idea of not wasting time, having fun, making my life easier and more; if doesn't work, simply doesn't work.

How many times do you open your closet and see that jacket or shoes (that if we are really honest, we know we are NEVER going to wear them) but then you think about the cost, or the person that gave us the present, and you prefer to leave it there or maybe someday you will get rid of it. (Most people - myself included - have something that meets those conditions and requirements, and we're afraid of get rid of them.) The problem is when it comes to productivity, and we think in terms of the cost instead of in terms of the utility. because in everything else we do, otherwise we will have got rid of many of those things I mention at the beginning of this paragraph.

It doesn't matter how much it cost, because the reality is that the cost of the potential wasted time, storage, and productivity is always going to be much higher. But we all carry that useless stuff that we wish would get lost, so you could buy the one you want, the one you should have gotten in the first place, the one that would had been useful. Open your bag, and throw that useless junk in the trash. (That's assuming that the bag itself should not go to the trash.) If doesn't work, it doesn't work. If it will work for someone else, give it away. But keeping things that don't work because they were expensive is not only a waste of space and time, it is wasteful.

17 - DON'T BE AFRAID OF SHORT-LIVED CONTEXTS

It isn't a secret that I have followed for many years the methodology of David Allen from his book Getting Things Done. My life has changed in many ways since 2003 when I first discovered that book. One of things that the book proposes is the use of contexts. A context is simply a tool, place, or person that you require to complete an specific action. During my years of practicing these principles, I have learned the power that these can contain, but it always surprises me how much fear people of these. (The idea of contexts seems to terrorize people; it is almost taboo, or it is like when there is a discussion of thermo-physics, and you don't understand anything about physics.) Many people think that a context is a rigid concept, that you can't change them and that you may need to maintain them forever. Other people think that they can only use the ones that are in the book. One of the most important tricks that I have discovered in this sense is to lose the fear to the short lived, temporary, context. @Before_the_trip, or @This_Weekend, or @Next_Week_in_Miami, are contexts as valid as @Home or @Computer.

The objective of a context isn't anything more than grouping tasks that should be done together with a tool, in a particular place, with a certain person, or in a situation. The first time that I discovered the power and importance of this trick was the first time I created a context called @Excel. I was super stressed, with more tasks on my list than I could accomplish, and it was one of those days when by the time I crossed something off as done, I had added five more things to do. I decided to take a few minutes to reduce my lists (or group them in a better way) so that each list had no more than ten items on it, so I could see them all on one screen. (At that time I had a Palm and the screen only allowed ten items at a time).

The first of these short-lived contexts that I worked with, was "@Excel." Three hours later, I had finished those ten tasks. (A list that I had thought was going to take me weeks to complete.) I was feeling on top of the world, but then came the question: now what do I do with this context? With a little fear, I deleted it. Two weeks later, I created it again when the chaos came back into my lists and experienced the same results that I had obtained before. Incredibly, the world didn't end, nor did my system fall apart if I created a context for only a few hours, days, or weeks. After that, I began using them when it was convenient, or as needed and without a doubt this has been one of the best tricks that I have learned. I am not afraid of having many of them in any given moment, but I am not afraid of deleting them. For me, contexts are to help me to see accurate steps, be more effective and faster and efficient, nothing more. If I could see all of the many actions on my lists once and choose accurately the correct one, I would not need these contexts.

Once I lost the fear I had and created many contexts, from the creation of contexts for special weeks, those ones for days that I need extraordinary concentration, even those for times that I need to prepare for an event.

One of those occasions was when, before a vacation trip, I made a list of the things that I wanted to think about and reflect on during that week. Instead of trying to fish them out of my system, I decided to create a context and take only this one piece of paper. That way, the rest of the system was going to stay untouched for those two weeks. It was the first vacation that I had taken in a long time, it was incredible. Not only that, but I was able to think fully and comfortably about the things on the list and when I came back to work, I was full of energy, more than after any previous vacation. I was able to make really important decisions. This continues being a practice that I do constantly, and as I said it's one of those tricks that has made a difference, not only in how I do the things, but the level of freedom of creation and elimination of these short-lived categories. @Before_Anniversary is a context as valid as @Home as @Reflexion or @Work.

Contexts are designed, as I see them, not to limit you, but to allow you to move even faster and accurately. The idea of them is to work with less resistance, so declare yourself free and eliminate or reduce the noise and the resistance that we all have in a way that works best for you. Don't think that there is a limit further than the one you set for yourself, don't think that there is only one set of valid contexts, other than those that you consider useful. In contexts, like in productivity and efficiency, the most important rule is the one that you create.

16: DON'T BE AFRAID OF THE DAILY TO DO LIST

For many people, the "today" list (@Today) is the best way they have found to handle their lives; for those who have read and practiced David Allen's principles from his book Getting Things Done, however, this is something that you're not supposed to do, something that people are afraid of, terrified even.

The daily list is a great help, under the correct principles, in my modest opinion. I have kept them many times, with a high grade of effectivity, but without a doubt, the success of it is in part because I have a set of rules:

1. The list needs to be created from an action in my system. (If I am adding something that it is not in my system, I first need to get it properly into the system.)

2. The list will NOT have more than 5 items. (If you finish those, you can always pick 5 more, but the idea of this list is to create the feeling of success, not more frustration.)

3. You need to be ready to throw this list in the trash and create a new one if the original conditions change. (This is the most important rule. Some people begin with the 5 items and then begin adding more. The idea of this list is to evaluate new inputs against this list. If a new item arrives that is more important than any of the five on the list, go back to step 1)

One of the reasons why many people are afraid of the daily list is simply that the list reminds them of those moments when they did the most urgent thing instead of the most important or the one that was going to generate more satisfaction. I firmly believe in working from a system and I firmly believe in a complete system. For many years I worked hard to create, maintain, and develop my system as my necessities and realities changed.

If in 2003 I had seen the system I have today, I would have thought that was impossible to accomplish it.

For me the daily list is much like a temporary context, but with special rules. The important part is to limit it (in my case to 5 things) and use the most important rule (Rule #3) and be ready to throw it in the trash and began a new one. This last rule is also the most difficult part. Once you create the list, in theory you've established the 5 most important actions of the day. That means that if you receive a call and someone requests something, this new development is going to be evaluated against those five things. Sometimes, this new input changes everything; in that moment, the secret isn't add item 6 to the list, but throw the list in the trash and get back to step 1. When we don't do that, the list ends up with ten or twelve items, and that's not exactly what we were looking for. This last part is important to reinforce, because it is one of the most important aspects of this list. Yesterday, I made one of my daily lists, and when I finished the third item, I discovered something much more relevant and important that what I was doing (sometimes it's something fun, that's valid, too, and counts) therefore I threw the list in the trash and proceeded to focus my attention to that. The big advantage of the Rule #1 in this case, as I complete items from the daily list I can mark those items as complete in my system whenever I get a chance to review. The unfinished "today" list can be tossed without concern of losing the remaining items--they're still in my system. In this case, when I threw out the daily list, I had completed three items, but two of those remained in my system, so I know they will not be lost. It is much easier to evaluate new information based on a clear perspective than against a mental chaos. The reason it was so easy for me to know the real importance of the new input was that I was comparing it against what I had defined earlier as the most 5 things for today, not against 10, 100, or 1000. There were only 5 (in fact two, because I had already accomplished three of the five.) Once I identified the new input, the list went to the trash and when I finish the new task, I went back to evaluate my day anew based on the new perspective.

15: CREATE A PORTABLE THINKING ENVIRONMENT

This is one of those dumb tricks, that has made a big difference and that has been great when I need to think, solve problems, concentrate, or simply write.

Have you ever stopped to think, "What do I need to think?" Which are your favorite elements that will make a perfect environment for thinking? Is a special kind of coffee? A glass of red wine? (Or maybe something more specific, like a glass of Rioja wine?) Music?

In my case, the indispensable thing is the music. (Coffee is always a great complement.) I have learned that music is what made thinking deeply portable in my case, and once I identified what it was what I like having to help me think, I carry it with me all the time. When I discovered the power of music for my thinking, I discovered that different artists and genres produce different effects. Beethoven's Nine Symphony, with the Berlin Philharmonic and Herbert von Karajan conducting is one of my favorites for thinking. It produces a tranquility in me and allows me to visualize things. I listen to Fito Paez, Joaquin Sabina, or Hombres G, as loud as I can when I am writing; the music recedes in the background, but when I get distracted, it makes easy for me to recover. When I need to improve my mood, I usually listen to the same playlist as for writing. Paco de Lucia playing Concierto de Aranjuez also allows me to relax. I understand that in my case music makes it easy to make thinking space portable, but I didn't always know what it was that I needed to think, work, and smile.

For some people, it's is a kind of tea or an specific pen, a keyboard that they only use for that kind of reflection, or a candle in front of the computer, or simply white noise.

For me, my portable environment for thinking and solving problems includes a tool for writing (in general, my iPhone or iPad, but in the past I used the Treo or the Palm) and the Beethoven's Nine Symphony directed by Herbert von Karajan with the Berlin Philharmonic. Not just any piece of music works for me, my needs are really specific, and it is always with me. If I am going to think, I only need my headphones and that Symphony, in many cases, really loud to block the external noise. I have tried classical music as a genre, thinking that any composition would do, but nothing else makes my brain enter the correct and adequate state. With the years, honestly, this discovery has provided me with great ideas and I can put it into effect in almost any part of the world or the city, even in my home.

To write is the art of creating and thinking; it doesn't matter if it is fiction or not, there is a certain kind of music that puts me in that magic place (that one defined by Mihaly Csikszentmihalyi in his book, Flow). It is a precise kind of music that allows me to isolate myself from the surroundings, the distractions, and creates the perfect environment (even if I am in the most imperfect place).

I would love to say that this is something that I discovered many years ago, but it is not like that. The good thing is now that I've identified it (and when I am not stubborn and decide to ignore even when I know better) I am able do things that in other moments are simply impossible and I get to work for hours and solve problems that otherwise might take me many more hours (and that I maybe wouldn't find the solution).

It is important to be able to think anywhere. In an ideal world all of us could hide away in the perfect room with a bottle of Port, dark chocolate, and a leather chair that still smells like new, with the perfect light and thick paper that not even Chinese ink will bleed through... If someone has a room like that and it is kind enough to lend it to me, I will bring the Port. But I don't have that kind of room, and I have never had it, but I have never not stopped thinking about that magical place.

In my case, that fantasy is not real, but I found something almost as good in a coffee house, outside waiting to pick my daughter at school, or on a morning when I was stressed out because things weren't moving forward like I believed they should. It is moments like these where the ability of putting my brain into thinking mode quickly is useful--incredible useful. Not so long ago, I was talking with another writer about this, and his answer was really interesting. To create his portable thinking environment, he drinks tea (and it's the only that that he does, otherwise he drinks coffee) and he removes his shoes. It doesn't matter where he is. In some way, the combination of the tea (even when it is bad tea) and his bare feet allows him to disconnect from his surroundings and get into that mind place where he can create stories. When I mentioned the music, he said that with music he would be singing and wouldn't be able to concentrate but while drinking tea barefoot, he can do miracles.

Think for a moment about what would be your perfect place to relax, think, write. Imagine it in detail. Then start to remove elements, if it is a white room, with a white leather seat, and a cup with something hot and steamy, begin eliminating details. What it is inside the cup, tea? Coffee? What kind of music? Is everything quiet? Work to get the perfect image. Look for the key element in what remains. Is it the chair or how you sit in it? Is it the silence or the fact that your eyes are closed? It is the color white or you could relax if the room was painted red instead? In my case it's always been music. In the case of my friend, it was a cup of tea and bare feet. What would your space have? What will make it portable?

14: HAVE MORE THAN ONE OF THE THINGS YOU CONSTANTLY USE

How many times have you arrived at the office and gotten the computer charger out of your bag? The iPhone cable? Those generic things you use daily? Worse yet, how many times have you forgotten the charger or the adapter at home?

This is one of those hidden costs that we tend to ignore; it is rare that I don't leave an item at home or at the office, or that it's happened only once. But every morning I crawl behind the desk to plug my laptop in, I then crawl behind to unplug it, and put it back in the bag. Try the following: measure the time that your daily routine takes you. In the morning, in the afternoon, at home. In less than a week, you will begin to accumulate hours. This doesn't take into consideration that you forget something and need to go back to get it before getting into the office (assuming you can arrive at the office after a certain time, many people can't). In my case, I discovered that connecting everything took around three minutes in the morning, disconnecting took two in the afternoon, I needed two minutes to set up at home and three before going to bed. That was a total of 10 minutes daily. One hour of my life per week. (Ok, 50 minutes from Monday through Friday and if I didn't move the machine on the weekend.) I asked myself if there was something I could do with an hour, and if an hour a week would make any difference, and how much it would cost me. In my case, the cost of the lost hour was much higher than the cost of a second charger and the cables. That same day I went out and got a complete set to have at home and left the other one in the office. At that time, I was traveling 80%-90% of the time, so I added a third set to my bag that I used only for travel.

On further reflection, I identified several more items that needed to be in duplicate or triplicate. Charger for the computer, I needed three: one in the bag, one in the house, and one in the office. Headphones for the iPhone: two; one in the pocket of my pants or shorts and one in the travel bag. There is nothing worse than when a pair of headphones gets damaged before a conference call that you know is going to be long. Pens, two. The one I always use, and the backup. (The back up is a cheap pen, but I replaced its cartridge with the same one my good pen uses. Even if I don't like the cheap pen that much, having the cartridge that I like means I will not be annoyed using with the backup pen if the good one gets lost.)

The savings in time and productivity are not always measured in hours per week, but in minutes of the day that add up without you even noticing them into hours per week. Saving ten minutes daily doesn't seems like a big thing, but that is an hour per week. Imagine that the opportunity that exists where you can save five to ten minutes. Imagine if you found twenty minutes daily this way... (Yes, that makes two additional hours per week. How about a nap on Saturday?) It is similar to when people discover that with $5 daily spent at Starbucks you could have bought the really expensive coffee machine you dream about and drink even more coffee daily.

There are other things, for which the long term cost is irrelevant, but the savings in productivity are incredibly high. When I was a frequent traveler (once upon a time, when I was traveling more than 160,000 miles per year), I had a full set of all the toiletries in my suitcase. When I arrived home, I didn't need to get it out of the bag unless it was to resupply or refill something that I had used up on the trip. Otherwise, it was a permanent fixture in my bag and always ready to go. In fact most of the things in that particular bag were duplicates and most of them never left that bag. Instead of thirty minutes every Sunday, I was able to pack my bag in less than ten. (An additional trick here: make a list of the things you always carry and never pack the bag from your memory; use your list.)

One of the things that you don't think about until you need it is an ethernet cable. Always carry one in your bag. The cost is close to zero, but it can save your skin (or make you the envy of the airport or the office you are visiting).

Here is a list of some of the things that, in general, we don't consider, but that their cost is minimal and the benefit incredible:

- Headphones for you iPhone (or whatever phone you use)

- Towel to clean your glasses

- Stamps and envelopes

- Backup pen (with the same cartridge and brand you like for your main pen)

- iPhone charger (one in the office, one in your bag, and one where the phone rests at night--that way you always have full battery)

- Extra batteries for those things that you carry (like a mouse or wireless keyboard)

- External keyboard. If you always type with an external keyboard make sure you have one in each place you work, including extra batteries.

- Deodorant and toothpaste Have two of each: the ones that you are using and one extra. That way when you begin using the replacement, you know you have time to buy more. There is nothing worse than waking up in a hurry and not having deodorant or toothpaste.

- Screw driver for your glasses (and extra screws)
- Pen drive. One in the bag, one at home, one in the office, plus the one that you always use.
- Medicine for headache, stomach upset, and acidity (Three sets: home, office and bag)
- ID (In your wallet and a copy in your bag.)

As you can see from this list (and I am sure there are more items that qualify), the monetary cost is really low, but the benefit is incredible high. Losing your ID can be a big problem if are traveling through an airport, but having a second ID can help. Almost nothing is worse that have a headache and needing to beg for an aspirin. Keep two tabs of the brand you like and you'll know that you have relief from your pain in the most effective way. The same applies to replacement batteries, they always fail when there is no replacement close by, otherwise they last forever.

There are many things that we use constantly and if you think for a moment before the crisis arrives, you can generate huge relief and incredible time gains. You gain productivity and efficiency not by looking for hours to save time, but in saving the wasted minutes and changing them into enjoyed minutes.

13: THE REFLECTION LIST

This list originated during the first real vacation that I took once I was working and my wife and I were fully independent adults. Before the trip, while reviewing my system, I made a list of the things that I would like to think on and reflect about, if I had the chance while we were enjoying the trip. I didn't want to open my system and see all the tasks until I returned, so I got a 3x5 index card and listed those things I would love to think about if the opportunity showed up. The opportunity showed up and I found that there's nothing better that fixing the world (or the little part that I have influence on) while gazing at the ocean and sipping a glass of Rioja wine.

The other thing I was carrying with me on that vacation was a pen and a Moleskine that I had brought in case I needed to write. This was so I wouldn't have to pull out my phone during the trip. I wanted to avoid the temptation of sabotaging my resting time or worse, that my wife would be mad at me because I had promised her that we were going to have a real vacation.

Not only was the experience incredible, but I was able to think without worrying about the tasks on my lists (and the many others than I wasn't aware of that were hovering over my head, bothering me). The experience was such a great one that I transformed the reflection list into something that it is part of my system and once a week, (sometimes even more than that) I open this list and spend some time thinking on these things. Sometimes items live on the lists for months, for no other reason other than I feel I haven't reflected enough and reached a conclusion.

The requirement for an item to be removed from this list is simple: I need to reach to the point at which I don't want or need to think or write more on that topic. Meeting this criteria can be difficult because, like most of the things you need to think and reflect on, fear always discourages me from continuing. That means I must determine if I've really finished or that fear doesn't want me to continue exploring the topic. Many times I have convinced myself that I have covered a topic, only to see it come back weeks or months later.

Recently (and for more than a year) this was one of the items on my list:

- What do you write? Fiction or productivity? Both? Neither?

It isn't a secret that I love to write fiction, but it isn't a secret that I love to talk about productivity. I am not looking to be a guru in productivity, that much I know, but without a doubt it's a topic that had been incredibly useful for me and from which I feel that I have many things to share. The problem was that I saw the two genres as contradictory and impossible to develop at the same time. I thought of writing one under Augusto Pinaud and the other A. Pinaud. But something about that wasn't working for me. Finally, while reflecting about it, I wrote the following:

"My name is Augusto Pinaud. I am a writer. Generally I write fiction and about productivity, maybe both are related."

It was a simple idea (born of many hours of thinking and meditation) but I finally understood that the limitation of doing just one or the other was established by fear and wasn't real. That was the day the idea for this book was born. The first draft was written in five days. It was like a a big weight was lifted; something that I didn't know I had nor that it existed inside me.

Even if it seems incredible, it wasn't until I read it in that one line, that for the first time I made peace with the fact that Augusto Pinaud is a writer. He writes in both genres, fiction and productivity. He hasn't discovered yet if the levels of productivity that he aspires to are fictitious or if it's that he finds time to dream on the stories that he writes thanks to the productivity.

Another item that was on my refection list was the question of why I refused to write in Spanish. I was born in Venezuela and didn't learn any English until I was 25 years old. (Before that I couldn't even ask for directions to get to the bathroom!) When I re-discovered the art of writing and decided to follow my adventure of being a writer, I refused to write in Spanish. Thanks to my list, I discovered the reason why but it took a long time; that was one of the items that spent many months on the list (in fact, I reflected on this topic for more than a year before resolving it). Others have been there for only one session.

Often, the items on the list will be simple things, because in general, you are having those thoughts and there are things that you are thinking on regardless. However, you don't usually give yourself time to sit and concentrate. In addition, there are topics that nag at you while at the same time, fear discourages you from taking those on, keeping you in that dark place where fear tends to imprison us. Fear continues winning many battles, but this list has allow me to win some, too, and discover incredible things about myself and the things I do.

The power of the reflection list for me has been invaluable. The reason may seem simple, but it is not. Do you remember that wrongly named "common sense?" This is another of those examples.

It's "common sense" that if you have a problem, you are going to sit and think about it. Yeah, right.

Even when you don't recognize it, you are thinking about those things, but instead of doing it in a focused way, you are doing it in a way that distracts you. As soon as you add that item to the list, you are giving yourself permission to focus your energies on the problem or the situation instead of expecting a miracle (or a simple random act) that will fix the problem. In my experience, the miracle or the random act always takes much longer and requires more energy than reflecting in a focused way.

12: DON'T PLAY WITH YOUR PRODUCTIVITY TOOLS

The tools you use to be productive (and to produce income) should not be used for play. Failing to give them the importance that they deserve not only is a mistake, but a mistake that can prove extremely costly.

Reinstalling all the software on your computer can take more than a day. Reinstalling Outlook after it gets corrupted can take many hours. (That is, assuming you have a backup; otherwise, not only will it take a lot of time, but the effects are catastrophic.)

Last year, a close friend of mine decided that he was going to update his computer, to have the latest operating system. The problem was that the operating system wasn't yet on the market, it was in beta. (Understand that during beta testing, the software is not yet ready for the public, it has errors, can cause problems, and it can fail.) The installation was flawless, and in a short time his computer was running the new operating system. There were small problems here and there, but nothing critical. For five days, everything was fine. The sixth day he was going to invoice his customers. The invoice software was incompatible with the new operating system. It didn't work. Within a few days, he reinstalled the old operating system so that he could continue to do business. This time, the installation wasn't so flawless as with the beta: the migration required much more work to put things back as they were before his "upgrade." What was the cost of playing with his system? Two weeks without revenue from the the invoices he was unable to send plus an uncounted number of hours reinstalling everything, copying files, and getting his machine ready so he could do the work he should have been doing all along.

Another example, comes from people who love productivity: playing with your task management system. Some folks move their tasks every week to some new software tool because it seems to have the characteristics that would have been useful the last week. How much time do they invest in switching systems? Untold hours poured into tools instead of the productivity the tools were intended to facilitate.

How much time are you spending playing with your system instead of using the system to be productive? How many hours in which you could have been productive or enjoying your the family or reading a book? Every hour you invest in changing things from software A to software B and then seeing how software B doesn't do that thing that we love in software A. Again, those hours are taking you away from something.

This is one of the things that people tend to forget: the time you spend playing and exploring is often wasted. (I am guilty of this, too. For many years, I spend hours playing with software and gadgets just because I was curious or thought they might someday prove useful.) Testing technology, software, hardware, and services can be addictive (and really fun) and it is a totally appropriate activity when you do it under the playing concept and not under the excuse of productivity. And more importantly, when there is no risk to damage your current tools for productivity or those that generate your income. It is this last piece the often slips by unnoticed: we install software and test services on the same computer that we will use later to accomplish our work and be productive. If nothing bad happens, it's perfect, but the risk is high. When we run into trouble, it's easy to miss that it was us that generated the problem to begin with! We blame the operating system, the hardware, or bad luck.

Just for the record, I am not saying that you shouldn't test software and hardware. What I am saying is that you should have a machine that is used solely to be productive and another for play. Rebuilding the play machine is never a big problem; rebuilding your productivity machine is always a big problem and often an emergency.

I realized this long time ago. For many years, I traveled with two PCs. (Partially with the excuse of having two monitors but one was for play and the other for work.) After the iPad was released, the iPad became my productivity machine. When the beta for iOS5 were available, for example, I was invited by a friend to try it. My friend, a programmer, wanted my opinion about a couple of things. I installed the new OS on my iPhone. When he found out, he ask me why I hadn't installed in the iPad, too, and I explained the principle of this chapter. Some time later, he got a second iPad, and when I asked him why, he told me: one to work, one to play. In that moment I knew, that I had taught someone a lesson that had been really important for me.

11 - GET A CHAIR. A GOOD ONE, I MEAN

On average, we spend six hours each day sitting, Monday through Friday, working. In general, we're sitting in a chair that provides little or no support; in many cases, you can't adjust it and it isn't even comfortable. In general, I am referring to the chair in your office. Unless you work for Google, where the chair is ergonomic (because they hope you will sit there a lot), most likely your chair costs, on average, $35 US. Many people, they place the blame on Human Resources, without noticing that the responsibility is only their own and not anyone else's. If you are not provided with the appropriate tools to accomplish your work, you need to find a way to obtain them.

For many years, I used one of those "comfortable" chairs that my employer was kind enough to provide me. When people began talking about working standing up, I made the switch immediately. My chair was really uncomfortable and standing up, without a doubt, was much better. Until then, I hadn't understood the significance of sitting for hours on something comfortable and I didn't learn that in the office; I learned it thanks to my home-office.

For a long time, I tried to set up a working space at home. I got desks (yes more than one) but always I end up working on the couch. There wasn't any way to find a place that was comfortable, so my home-office always ended up being the spot to put all those things that I didn't want to deal with. I even got a couch and put it in my home-office with the intention of keeping myself in there longer and being able to justify having it. The couch made me stay in the room, but I wouldn't get close to the desk. The most successful desk in my home-office was the one I used to work standing up.

It was many years later that we had someone visiting us for three months and I had to leave my home-office (so it could be a guest room) and work at the dining room table. I began working there for hours. Once our visitor left, I moved back to my home-office. Twenty five minutes later, I was in the kitchen making coffee. That was the first time that I considered that the problem wasn't the room, it was The Chair.

I could not believe that the whole problem had been something that simple. I had bought tools, monitors, keyboards, tables, accessories but I had never got anything else that the cheap Target chair and, later, a folding one.

I took one of the chairs of our dining room table and put it in the room that I had failed for many years to use as a home-office. The next three days I worked like never before in that room. On the following Friday, my wife asked me to return the dining room chair and I got back my old chair. I wasted that Friday: I wasn't able to concentrate, I drank coffee, water, went to the bathroom, sorted stuff, but didn't sit a moment to do what I was suppose to do.

Monday morning, I moved the dining room table chair back and learned that I needed a comfortable chair, where after five hours I wanted to remain seated. What I'd been looking for all along was a place where I didn't get tired working, but honestly until that moment I never thought about the chair. Believe me, if I had understood that earlier, I would have happily paid for the chair that would have allowed me to work comfortably for many hours. It wasn't that I didn't want to work, it was that I was unable to stay put for enough time to be useful.

That was the moment I replaced all the chairs in my life--the ones that I use to work--with comfortable chairs that I can spend hours sitting in without lose my focus. I continue using the couch from time to time, but not because I can't stand the chair, but because at times, the couch is the appropriate place to be. But since I discovered the chair, I can spend uncountable hours sitting there, where the distraction may occur but not because of the discomfort from the chair I'm seated on.

I continue enjoying doing certain things standing up, but I do most of my work seated, in a good and comfortable chair, that allows me to be seated there more than eight hours without feeling as if I've been there that long. Before you mention it, I am aware that this seems to be "common sense" but again, it wasn't common sense for me. Also, if it is such common sense, how is possible that there are so many people sitting in so many crappy chairs? People who have serious back problems and other sufferings, that have never allowed themselves to buy their own chair that allows them to diminish discomfort or even eliminate the sufferings they have. Of course, it's "common sense." That's the reason I didn't consider the chair as the problem. Regardless, the important thing is to evaluate the chair where you are sitting, where you spend many hours. Is it appropriate? Does it cause you pain? Maybe is time to get out and get one real chair, one that's good and comfortable.

10: PLAN THE SIMPLE THINGS

When people begin planning and organizing, they think about the big projects, and block time slots out of their days, for the many hours they need to write the big novel. They often ignore the simple things and the simple stuff.

In my opinion, organizing and planning for the "dumb" and small things is exactly what allows me plan for those big and important things. This is another of these tips learned recently... How useful this would had been ten years ago!

I don't write everyday. I have days that I do other stuff (simple and not important) so when I get to write, I can focus my attention on the writing. That is, instead of trying to work on my book project while my mind is reminding me that we don't have milk, or coffee is running out, or that I haven't made the appointment with the pediatrician.

For many years, I thought that I could do both (the big project and the smaller stuff) during the day, and recently I realized that if I eliminate the noise of those simple and less important tasks, I can focus and work at incredible levels.

To be effective and really enjoy highly focused time, it's important to plan for the small stuff. For many years, on my calendar have been three kind of appointments: my lunch time, time to take care of email (at least two sessions of 30 minutes a day in which the objective is get to inbox zero), and last, three hours for my weekly review and my extraordinary hour. The people who know me know that dealing with me when I'm hungry is a bad idea, therefore it's important to me to not get hungry. For that reason, my lunch hour has been a priority for which I block time. If you want to meet with me at that time, then we need to meet with food in front of us. With email it's the same. Most people think that email is one of those things that you'll find a way to deal with. The reality is that in many jobs, answering and checking email is as important as sitting in the meetings which you have to attend for political reasons. So you need to plan to sit with email, in the same way you set aside time for the meetings. In my experience, most people need an hour to maintain control over their email. Thirty minutes at the beginning of the day and thirty at midday. (Many people also need an additional thirty minutes more at the end of the day.) If you do the math, subtracting the number of hours it takes you to do email and sit in meetings, you will see that you are expected to do your job in two and a half hours a day. That includes socializing, lunch, and bathroom breaks.

I used to block time to do all the little things over the course of the week, but recently, I have concentrated them into a day or two, and the result has been incredible. It turns out that those little things are the ones that turn into emergencies, which you can't avoid any longer and that now require your attention. Often, those little things are the ones that don't allow us to give the attention that we really need to the important stuff. Those little things are the ones that demand your attention when you are really busy with a project or an important task. Here is where we allow procrastination to win. We are waiting until the moment we are in the mood to take of those little things but that hour never arrives. It's not until that "dumb" activity becomes an emergency that we think about all those times when we could have taken care of it in twenty minutes instead of when it becomes a crisis that costs us an hour. In most cases we don't even notice that that it's the little thing that had been distracting us for weeks, maybe even even months.

Filing, paying bills, organizing files on the computer, taking the dogs to the veterinarian, updating software, updating the computer, changing the hard drive that is making a weird noise. All of these are tasks that are simple, but we never plan the time to accomplish them. All of these are examples of activities that we can do in minutes but in crises, become tasks that require hours.

Just about everybody has planned to take a day to work on something important. We've spent days removing all the obstacles so we can get the most out of that time we are protecting. We've all experimented and tasted those days. They taste like success, and you remember them for a long time afterward. The interesting thing (and I am also guilty of this) is that we don't do that consistently. We taste success with a satisfied smile, when we do it, but for some reason that I don't understand, we don't do it regularly. Once I began to plan these focused days regularly and made sure that the "dumb" things were handled in advance, the results began to show in a way that I wasn't expecting.

If there is one thing I've learned, and I hope that I can teach to someone, it's the value of planning for the little things so you can clear your focus and your attention for when you sit to accomplish the big things. Not all projects or tasks are equal, that we all know, so why we do we insist in treating them as if they where? Next week, plan to spend at least half a day cleaning and doing the "dumb" and small things that are bothering you. Then spend the other half working on something important. The experience will be incredible.

9: ALWAYS CARRY YOUR READING MATERIAL

Even with the availability of smart phones, iPads, eBooks, and other electronics, I am always in awe how many people sit in waiting rooms with the hope that they will find among the magazines available, something interesting to read. This happens even though at home, they had that magazine that they really wanted to read, or the novel that they were reading last night until one in the morning. In many cases, it's true that we don't open the magazine, instead we play Angry Birds or something important like that, while the pile of things to read just grows and grows, until we simply quit and stop trying to read it. This last bit is the sad part. All those people have stuff that they are intending to read, books that they have tried to read for months and magazines that are piled up at home. Having something you want to read with you is an act of efficiency.

Even when I was reading paper magazines, I used to take them to the doctor's office and dump them there once I finished with them, or I took a book. Today I take books or those things that I want to read from blogs or the internet in Instapaper. I always have something to read that I am interested in and that helps me to read all those things in the reading pile.

For many years one of my annual goals was to read more than 52 books. (And I've been very successful: 54 in 2011, 71 in 2010, 55 in 2009. Sadly, I didn't keep records prior to 2009.) When the people ask me how I am able to accomplish that much reading, I answer with the fact that I always have a book with me. Fifteen minutes of waiting in the doctor's office transform themselves into fifteen minutes of reading. Waiting outside my daughter's school is between ten and twenty minutes of reading; her dance class, fifty minutes of reading. We all have those spaces where we can read, it's just that the book or the magazine or the article is waiting for us in another place.

Waiting (and we all wait many hours) with the hope that we will find something interesting that will bring us closer to our dreams and objectives is like finding a bottle in aisle four of the grocery store than will make your day last twenty-five hours. I am sure that someone in some waiting room has found an article that has changed their life, but in general I assume that it was the exception more than the rule. Usually, we simply spend the waiting time looking at magazines that we are not interested in, looking for an article that help us pass the time instead of the book we were reading last night, that kept us up until three in the morning, and we can't wait to get back to reading.

Again, it's one of those silly things that we've all done, but it is unproductive. To be efficient and productive requires thinking about the little things. The ideal would be to have four hours in which no one will interrupt us, but I don't recall when was the last time I had one of those four hour blocks. Can you?

Do you want to increase the number of things you read? Learn to take something with you, something you are genuinely interested in or something you want to learn or to write about. Stop believing that luck will help you to find the right article: bring it with you. If you don't want to carry the whole magazine, tear out the two or three articles you want, and bring only those pages.

8: REDUCE YOUR DAILY LOAD

When was the last time that you checked all the "necessities" that you carry in your wallet and in your bag?

Things tend to get into your bag and stay there, and suddenly you notice that it's incredible heavy. In my experience, there are three things that are in every bag or wallet.

1.- The things that we should have in multiples so you don't have to carry them. (Flip back to Tip 14 to learn more about which items you should consider.)

2.- Things that should not be there anymore. (Like that pen that has no ink, the toy you picked up in the car a week ago and that you haven't returned to your kid.)

3.- The things that used to belong there, but not anymore. (Like the insurance cards that have expired or the extra battery for the cell phone that we don't even have anymore.)

Once a week, you should empty your bag (as well as your wallet) and consider what should return and what should stay out. Bringing everything with you in case you might need it doesn't help you, and it can damage your health, even if though that may sound sound incredible.

Many years ago, I began having terrible back pain. (For the ones that knew me then, it's true that I was overweight, but regardless, the back pain wasn't normal.) When I got to the doctor and explained my problem, before trying anything else, he observed me. Before he told me the obvious (that I was overweight) he ask me to get my bag. Before he weighed me, he weighed the bag. I remember was 20kg (44 lbs)! I was carrying everything that I might need.

His prescription was simple: "You need to carry less stuff or get a bag with wheels." He charged me for the visit and each one of us continued on his way.

Immediately, I purchased a bag with wheels. (Ok, took me a few days until I was able to relax since I was really mad at him. Once I relaxed, then I followed his advice.) The sad part was, that as soon as I stop putting the weight on my back, the back pain disappeared. Did I mention that I was mad, and did not completely believe the doctor? But took me years to understand that I needed many fewer things than the ones I used to carried constantly. It's easy to get caught thinking that the world will end if you don't have the things that might be useful. The reality is that we rarely use this stuff and when we need them, the bag is in the car and we find we can do without.

We have all carried an incredible number of useless things, things that we thought that might be useful, and without a doubt are useful, just not all the time.

These days, once a week, I pull everything out of my bag. Those things that I have not used are evaluated to see if they should be kept there or not. The result is a small bag that weighs practically nothing. Often, this allows me to only carry only the iPad and very little else. I have purchased accessories that I am sure would not be considered"indispensable," but after considering the weight and reducing what I carry all the time, my bag today weighs almost nothing. I don't ask myself anymore how people manage with a small bag; I'm trying to learn what else I'm carrying that is unnecessary.

7: WRITE DOWN THE KEY INFORMATION - THE KEY LISTS

When was the last time that your printer ran out of ink? Exactly when you needed to print that urgent document and you ended up running to the store. You reached the store, thinking you knew your printer model but as soon as you saw the ink (sometimes in a wall full of options), you forgot the brand and discovered that you can't buy it because honestly, you have no idea which one. Sometimes you can grab your cellphone and ask someone to check for you. But most of the time, you have to take a deep breath, drive back, write the model on a sticky note, and go back to the store. Now you are able to buy the correct cartridge (while your stress is increasing proportionally to your bad mood), run back and finally print that important document. And once this is done, and the document is ready, the sticky note ends up in the trash can. But after a certain number of pages, you will simply repeat the story. In an earlier chapter, I mentioned that I keep an extra set of ink cartridges, but I repeated this tale for many years before that. That's the reason I know this story so well.

We all like to think that we will not do something like this, and instead be like those people that effortlessly remember the correct printer model. For years I envied the people that could do that, that reached the store and knew exactly the model of their printer, the labeler, and the special type of bulb that their refrigerator uses. I thought that it was impossible for me to do something similar. Later I discovered that these folks don't have incredible memories. Their secret is writing the information down and keeping the list available for the future, for when they are going to use it. The secret was not to get rid of the sticky note but to process it into the system so the next time that information is needed, it's available. What a big difference! This is one of those simple things that over time, produces incredible results. Imagine only one trip to the store when you need a new ink cartridge... or to buy a special bulb for the bathroom fixture because the light produced will be beautiful.

It was 2004 when for the first time I made a list with this kind of information. I can't describe the emotion nor the feeling of success that it produced in me when I got to the store and instead of getting mad, not find the sticky note, and not having to call anyone, I open my Palm and searched: "Printer." The result: Cannon BJ-10! I was reminded and smiled. It was one of those moments when I discovered that the simple and "dumb" things can make my life incredibly better. For the first time, buying an ink cartridge was something easy.

One moment, my wife is asking for the dimensions of the dining table... yes, the ones that includes the leaves. The next moment, I have them for her and the problem of getting a new tablecloth is solved. This time the info was in my notes on the phone; there was no need for a sticky note (or to return home to take the measurement). In the past, two things would had happened. First, we would have guessed at the dimensions and bought the table cloth. And second, it would have been the wrong size necessitating another trip to the store to get the correct size (most likely without the correct measurement even this second time). We'd end up buying another one hoping that it is in the correct size or we go back home take the measurements and return to get it. My wife and I have made all these trips. More than once. Now, we have learned to take measurements and keep them on a note in our phones.

It is incredible the amount of stuff that we don't write down, but having the correct information would save us many times in which we try to guess measurements or models or battery sizes. My objective with this trick is not to use my brain to remember useless information (like the model of the printer or labeler) and use it for things a little bit more useful (like the next novel).

These are some of the things in my system:

- Model of the printer (-Inventory numbers of the black and color cartridges)
- Model of the labeler
- Batteries for the remotes at home (TV, Roku, Apple TV, garage door openers, the wireless keypad that opens the garage)
- Dimensions of the kitchen table
- Kind of battery that the lamp in the grill uses
- Mouse and external keyboard battery sizes
- Dimensions of the furnace filter
- Measurements of the water filter
- Dimensions of the couch (height, width, depth)
- Dimensions of my desk
- Carbon monoxide sensor batteries
- Kinds of special bulbs (bathroom, kitchen, fridge)

It isn't that I spend my day looking for this information, I just write it down when it's relevant, but instead of a sticky note, it's a durable, easy to find note in my phone. Now I have a lot of information that if I need to buy a replacement of one of those things, it's easy and I guarantee that I will do it in only one trip. Do you know the model of razor that your husband or wife uses? My wife doesn't tell me buy me a razor X color Y. She just ask if I can buy her a razor. That info is in the appropriate place, on the list. In my experience she doesn't know the particulars either, she just recognizes the right brand and type when she sees them in the store.

Of course a couple of weekends ago, we discovered that we didn't have the measurement of the windows in my daughter's room. We bought the wrong curtains. (I didn't say that we are perfect; we are not even close.) But now we have the dimensions of that window and the other ones that want new curtains for. This tip has nothing to do with not doing dumb things; it is just try to do them no more than once each!

6: THE TWO BROWSERS

The tale of the two browsers was discovered when my job changed to be online most of the time and my list of tasks simply grew and grew... If I remember correctly, it was around 2006 or 2007 when my job evolved. I was handling accounts in Latin America, the US, and Canada. For hours, I reviewed prices and marketing campaigns in those three markets. It was really fun, but my job was in an environment in which I was easily distracted all the time.

Obviously I was doing something wrong. I was spending many hours in front of the computer, but I felt like I wasn't doing my job. So I tried a software called Rescue Time.

The results were alarming: I was spending hours on the

computer but the majority of that time wasn't on sites where I needed to be for work. Instead, I was hanging out in forums, blogs, and participating in online communities. Obviously, I needed a solution, the faster, the better.

I don't remember how I got to the idea of the two browsers or if I read it somewhere, but it was the most simple solution. I installed Chrome from Google and kept Safari (Apple's browser). The only change was one simple rule; that changed forever the rules of the game and had helped me accomplish incredible things.

I was allowed to waste all the time I wanted, but only in Safari. When my internet surfing was work related, I worked in Chrome. Everything related to work or producing income: researching clients, competitors, prices, marketing campaigns, and access inventories were done using Google Chrome. Reading blogs, participating in forums, writing on my blog, reading about technology, wasting time, all done in Safari.

The result was incredible and instantaneous. I didn't stop reading blogs or forums. No, I continued accessing those forums and blogs, but in a different way. I wasn't wasting hours without noticing but everyday, every moment, was a more conscious decision. When I was doing my job, that was done in Google Chrome and was much better. I remained more focused and was much more effective. With time, my brain and my subconscious became trained to play in the Safari park and to work on the Chrome office. Each time that I navigated to a "play" site in Chrome (43Folders.com, TaraRobinson.com, The DavidCo Forums, my Google reader), my subconscious reminded me that I should use Safari instead. That was the moment when the incredible was happened. In many cases, I was telling myself, "Later," and I went back to work. Other times, I just moved to Safari and I set an alarm to remind me to return to Chrome. At some point, I learned the psychological reason this worked so well for me: my brain began to associate how Chrome and Safari work and I began associating Chrome with work and Safari with play.

As I said earlier, the result was incredible in that when I began using the iPad as my primary machine, I noticed that I was needing another browser. I installed iCab Mobile for work and continued with Safari for play. Recently, I replaced iCab Mobile for Chrome for the iPad, a much better browser.

Over the years, I have recommended this trick to many people and it works well except in those work situations where you're not allowed to install additional software. (In that case, my recommendation is don't go to any off-topic site, because most likely your employer can see and record every step you are making online.) Of the people who have implemented this trick, they have enjoy the same results I have, as well as an increase in their productivity.

Many times, to eliminate an undesired behavior, it is enough to give the brain a cue that it is doing something incorrect. No one wants to waste hours on the web when you have many tasks to do and, in general we don't notice those wasted hours. We don't acknowledge where they went, we don't know how many there are, we believe that we've spent only five minutes and in reality was three or four hours wasted.

This trick works much the same as when my dogs hear the sound produced by a can of compressed air; they know that they are doing something wrong. It is simple and effective (and not in any way cruel to the animal). The only problem with this cue is when I'm using the compressed air to clean something. My dogs freak out and have no clue what they're doing wrong. For me, opening Google Reader in Google Chrome produces the same effect; my brain immediately hears the same sound as the compressed air makes, and a change of browser is in order. It is exactly in that instant, that I can make a better choice. I can decide: am I going to read blogs or will I work more? Is it that I am thirsty and because of that I am losing focus or do I really need to hang on and finish my job? The cue for this choice is simple, and the effect is incredibly powerful.

It doesn't matter which browser you use to play and which one to work. The important thing is to begin and use both. In cases where it is not possible to install a second browser, my recommendation is use your smartphone for play when you're on "their" computer. IT has the ability to know what sites your machine has visited, how many hours and minutes you were on Facebook or reading blogs, and it's information that any manager can request (and in many working environments, it's enough to get you fired). If the problem is that the job that you should finished in four or five hours is taking you twelve because you spend seven on Facebook, install a second browser and establish the rule: "I can only use this browser to work not to play." Back when Amazon was one of my customers, and I visited Amazon.com for work, I always used Chrome; when it was to buy stuff, I used Safari.

My brain is used to this distinction now and well trained, and this simple trick has made a big difference beginning when I discovered it, the day that I began telling the tale of the two browsers.

5: DISCOVER YOUR WARNING SIGNS

We all have warning signs, but most of us tend to ignore them. These are the emergency symptoms, those things that we all do when we begin to lose our center of balance in our priorities, when we are going from our normal state to stressed and survival mode. When you continuously ignore these warning signs, your body tends to go to preservation and defense, and that it is not the most productive state to be in and never will be.

One of my most obvious symptoms is that I stop reading. (I've asked my friends to point it out to me if I am not talking about a the book I am reading. When I'm stressed, I don't have the ability to notice what's gone missing.). Among the people I love, their symptoms vary; some begin to sleep more, others to walk, some begin looking for "needs" to buy, and still others discover that they spend the whole Saturday reading in bed.

The symptoms tell you that something is not ok. Sometimes it's just fatigue but it can be stress or fear, as well. The important point is to be able to identify them and know what they mean so you can act before reaching critical levels. At least identify that these red flags exist, even when you're unable to find out what's causing them to occur, so you'll know that something is happening and be able to focus your attention where it's needed most.

For example, when I get stressed out, the first thing I do is to quit reading. I am busy, I rest less, stop taking the small breaks during the day, begin to look for ways I can work faster and also I begin to pressure myself to accomplish things in less time. Sadly, the faster I am trying to go, the slower I am. It's ironic, but that's how it is. If I don't recognize the warning signs fast enough, I run out of energy, and, eventually, I collapse. The problem is not hurrying up and accomplishing more. The problem has two elements. The first is that I want everything done right away, and it's not just one thing on the list. Because I want it all done now, I always end up in frustration and which puts me into a vicious circle, one from which I never escape in good condition. The second is that the more I push, the less capacity I have. The reason to take the breaks and relax the mind isn't because you're lazy, it's to guarantee that when you need to confront a problem, you're in the best mental state. Think about it: How many times have you stayed late at the office, tired but trying to finish something instead of going home to rest and recover? In my experience, nine out of ten times that I've done this, the next morning I was back doing over the things I'd stayed late to do. And generally with higher quality and in a lot less time. If I am rested, I can complete the same work in a shorter amount of time. If I had just gone home and rested appropriately, I would have finished my project much more quickly, than when I stayed late the night before.That's one of the reasons the warning signs are important: by heeding them, you'll save lots of time and energy.

Pizza. Pizza is another warning sign that generally indicates that I'm tired. When all that I want to eat is pizza (lunch and dinner, breakfast doesn't matter). It is an special feeling, hard to describe here, but I know when I feel it, my body is asking for pizza. And it means that my level of fatigue is reaching critical levels. My body asks for pizza as if it were indispensable for its survival. In the past, I'd give in to the craving and eat pizza (the biggest one I could find) but without understanding why. Today I know it is a symptom and even when I go ahead and give in, I understand that I need to slow down, rest, or even go to bed and forget everything else. I love pizza; all that I have learned is that when the craving shows up, it's a warning sign so I can take the correct measures. I have been able to identify some of mine, and some of the people close to me. When the warning sign shows, in most cases I am able to help others to do what is important, rest, in many cases.In the past, when I didn't realize what my craving meant, I just devoured pizza day after day (five in a row is the worst I remember, from Tuesday to Saturday. And on that Saturday, I collapsed and rested. If I hadn't, maybe it would had been six days.) What are your warning sings? One of my friends stops her daily walks. We've been friends so long that I have the freedom to ask and even instruct her to go out and walk. (This same friend has sent me off to read many times; it's something reciprocal we do for each other.)

I have another friend that begin looking for a fight. He gets ultra sensitive, stops reading, opens the liquor bottle. Usually my friend drinks very little but when he gets home and wants a whisky, it's a stress sign. Before he realized this was a warning sign, he would have one or two or three drinks. Now that he recognizes it for what it is, he goes and gets some exercise instead. Personally, I am not ready for something as serious as exercise, but I am willing to identify which of those symptoms affect my productivity, which is my normal state, and avoid reaching those critical levels where recovery take days instead of a few hours. But it's not only that we don't recognize the warning signs. Even with the warning signs, we don't always know how to avoid reaching the critical level, or we think that it is impossible to stop and rest, and that the critical level is impossible to avoid.

Often, identifying your own warning signs is really hard and sometimes, it's impossible. This is why you should include people around you who can help you to identify what's happening and be sure that you're not ignoring your warning signs. Once someone else has helped you to identify some of them, it's easier to notice them the next time. One of the most important things, besides getting good at identifying your own warning signs, is to become familiar with your loved ones' warning signs. Being able to identify those allows you to help them to avoid reaching their own critical states. There is a popular saying: Meditate twenty minutes a day; unless you are busy, in which case meditate for an hour. This is the essence of identifying your warning sings: discovering when to meditate twenty minutes and when you need an hour.

4: PLAN FOR PRODUCTIVE AND FOCUS TIME

All of us, at one time or another, have blocked our schedules and spent that time to move an important project forward. Most likely, you have accomplished incredible results that way. During your focused time, you were probably incredibly productive and worked with extra focus. You have even reached the mythical place that Mihaly Csikzentmihalyi talks in his book, Flow: The Psychology of Optimal Experience.

In general, these periods are super effective, too. You have finished big projects, discovered things that you thought impossible, clarified situations that seemed impossible to clarify, and worked as if the world around you didn't exist.

I have not yet met a single person who, after blocking some time to focus and having experienced the feelings of success and accomplishment that this focused time produces, doesn't recognize its value. Sadly, I know only a handful of people who make taking this kind of time a priority.

We all know the value; we all admit its importance. How wonderful it is when you have moved that project forward. How incredible that Thursday was or that afternoon. But only a handful of people do it consistently. Why? The answer is simple. Because they have not yet discovered the importance of planning to have productive time. Yes, it is that simple. (You can add this to the famous list in Trick #22... yep, that one about common sense.)

As Trick #10 was planning for the little things so things gets done before they transform into emergencies, it's just as important to plan to have productive and focused time.

Many of us organize our tasks in contexts and in multiple lists. We have simplified, eliminated, and reduced the excess, but we haven't stopped and planned to be productive. In many cases, we have searched for ways to do more in less time, but not necessarily more of the important stuff. What is the use of crossing one hundred things from a list, if the only important project hasn't moved forward or gotten anything marked on it as done? In general, we plan many things, but we also sin in not planning the little things (Trick #10) and use this trick for something more important: planning consistent productive and focused time. Time when you are going to focus your energy and accomplish only one thing.

It seems as if we're hoping that this time will magically show up in our calendars or in our days. A few us of us have been so fortunate that this happy accident has occurred. The problem is that when this miracle occurs, like when two hours show up because the customer cancels the meeting, instead of leaving the time blocked and working those two hours on a key project, we run to read some blogs, dink around on Facebook or Twitter, or pick an action that it is going to be a cheap win. In other words, we waste that miracle.

Even if you recognize the benefit of having this kind of planned, focused, productive time, you have a hidden fear of blocking the time. It's easy to be afraid that the people will think that you're not available. Some people go so far as to attend more than one conference call at the same time, one on their cellphone and one on the office phone, just so people don't think that they can't accomplish all. The addiction to stress is so much bigger than the idea of moving things forward, confronting the project is an idea that is more terrifying than finishing it, therefore we don't plan to have those hours in which we can disconnect the internet, email, phone and, in a certain way, the world. Play some music, get it loud and for two or three hours, nothing gets to be more important than the project you have in your hands.

Like I said at the beginning, the most interesting thing is that many of the people I know have done this at some point. Disconnected the internet, turned the cellphone off, placed the phone on DND (Do Not Disturb), closed the door of the office, played their music on their iPhone or iPod, placed a sign on the door, and, with the biggest guilty feeling, focused their energy on their most critical project. At the end of that time, most of them come out feeling great, full of happiness, enjoying that they finished the project that seemed impossible to finish... the experience was incredible, the results amazing. The incredible part, though, is that we don't do anything to make this experience something more regular in our lives. Instead, we get out our yellow book, that one that we have full of excuses, and get back to enjoying our favorite addiction, the addiction to stress.

It is not that we didn't experience the value of those hours of high productivity and focus, it's that we're terrified that others might think that we need to block time to do the things we need to do. We're terrified that if we do this constantly we aren't going to be stressed out like other people; we are going to stop belonging to the group and we are not going to be invited to the club house anymore. We are terrified that other people might think that we can accomplish more than one thing at the time. We are terrified that others might discover that we are trying to take time to make progress on those projects and that we consider those to the most important ones, telling to the rest of the world that it can wait;

definitely an idea that for many, is absolutely terrifying.

Now comes the challenge, a simple one... Look for four hours in the next three weeks. Block out everything. Plan to spend those four hours only on projects of high impact. The fourth week don't block the time, but spend some time considering if your focused time was worth the effort... The next week (the fifth one) is when you are going to discover the impact... I am willing to assure you that after this experience you are going to begin to find the time. For many years, I arrived at the office one hour earlier that my peers; most days I was able to do more in that hour (related to high impact projects) than during the rest of the day.

3: GIVING YOURSELF TIME AFTER A TRIP TO CATCH UP

For some reason, there are activities and people that you will give the time that you don't have, without conditions, reserves, or limits. Even more interesting, giving yourself a little bit of this generosity is almost impossible to even consider.

Before I explain, let me tell you three stories. The first one is from a person who needed to leave work for a week to take care of her mother who was sick. Without hesitation, she took the time, even took two extra days to guarantee that her mother was well cared for. Most of us would had done the same.

Now let's think about replacing a manager in another city.

Monday morning, you run to an airport, get on a plane, and work in the other office for two weeks. When the manager returns to work, you go home, back to your regular job. During that time you have been doing your work and the work of of the person you were replacing.

Finally, imagine the sales person, who travels 90% of the time. That means that, more or less, he is in the office only one week of the month. He begins traveling on Monday morning and returns on the Thursday night, after working all week, and on Friday, he tries to get to the office.

The problem with these three examples is that in none of these cases are these people giving themselves the chance to catch up or organize themselves to make good decisions. Without a doubt, the woman taking care of her mom would have extended her trip has her mom needed her. The same was true for replacing the manager: if they needed another week, you'd have been there. But in none of these examples did they consider recovery time, not in the personal sense, but time to get back into the hurricane that means returning to the office the very next day.

Let me begin declaring myself guilty. I was just as guilty of not factoring in recovery time until I understood that to be really effective, I needed to know where I was going and that sometimes, I needed that time to catch up. I was on a flight returning home once when the flight attendant said, "If the oxygen mask is deployed, please put on your own mask before trying to help others." I had heard this announcement millions of times before, but it was that day when I understood that to really help others, finish my job efficiently, give the 100% of myself and my work, it was important to take care of myself. Otherwise, I was risking not only not being able to help others, but the probability that I was going to need help myself. Sadly, I have observed friends and family burning out, exhausted, and sick because they didn't stop for a moment to take care of themselves. They didn't take the three additional hours that they needed for rest after a week of taking care of family, or traveling overnight to be at the office the next morning, not only wasting time, but without thinking about it, creating conflicts that were unnecessary.

We have all been in one or more of the three situations, when someone needs us, covering for someone at work, or changing a plane ticket because we had an important meeting. We have all done those things for someone else. But only a few of us stop and take time for ourselves. The time to slow down, reorganize yourself, and confront things, not from the point of view that nothing happened, but assuming, understanding, and comprehending that it is as necessary and as important to take time to get back up to speed before we jump into the hurricane that we have ahead.

Imagine, for a moment, an airplane. To fly, it is necessary that it gets speed and momentum on the runway. Now imagine that the plane doesn't have fuel or a runway to gain speed and momentum. What will happen?

Exactly the same thing that will happen to you if you were an airplane and you return from these kinds of events and don't allow yourself to recover and recharge your energy. You need to check all the emails, bills, papers on the desk and the other stuff that have arrived to your world during that time.

That is exactly the issue, and where we tend to fail and make a mistake. We return from these unexpected situations, or even vacations, but we don't give ourselves the chance to recover, to prepare for the days ahead, even when, without a doubt, we would have taken extra days for events like the ones I described earlier. At the end of three days, it seems like we need to be hospitalized in order for us to recover.

In my experience, if instead of trying to jump into the chaos that we left, if we took a day or even half a day to organize and plan, we could be as effective as the airplane at the end of the runway, full of gas and with favorable wind... It is exactly for that reason that I do the impossible, and plan with that image in mind. Even when I was traveling more than 90% of the time, I blocked time to recover, to avoid crashing, and for many years (and with varying levels of success) I have recommended that people close to me learn to do the same. It is easier to take a day to recover than the seven you'll need in two weeks time when your body forces you to stop.

Obviously, it's not always possible to take time to recover. But even when you don't acknowledge and believe it, thinking that unlike the airplane, you don't need that much gas or runway to take off, the reality is still there. Someone once told me, "I can get gas while I'm flying; I don't need the runway for landing or taking off, I don't have time for that." Eventually you are going to have to have fuel and you are going to be forced to land to get it. The question is how are you going to do it: with enough runway or with the emergency sirens waiting to greet you.

2: DEFINE YOUR DESTINATION. IN WRITING AND IN DETAIL

It isn't enough to define what you want to obtain. It is important that you to define it in detail and in writing. Where you are going and where you are headed is something that changes and evolves over time. For example, if you take the test to find out how fast you type and discover that your speed is 20 words per minute, you might decide that it's important to improve and set a goal to improve to 40 words per minute. If instead of writing it down, "Learn to type 40 words per minute", you write "learn to type faster," you will know the direction you are taking but most likely you never will not discover that you get there.

Life happens, you practice some, improve a bit and then forget the goal. Ten months later, you might decide to get the goal back on track, take the test again. Now you find that you type 33 words per minute. Your new goal will never be 40 words per minute since that seems like it isn't enough, so you think you should aim for 66 words per minute.

In this case, the problem isn't that the goal changes, the problem is that you never got the satisfaction of reaching your initial goal and most likely won't get the joy of reaching any other, either.

In this little example, it may seem as if it is of little importance, but imagine what happens when there are ten, fifteen or twenty things that you are never going to accomplish! Most people wonder why they get so frustrated in their pursuit of their New Year's goals. Some give up altogether and stop setting goals entirely.

This doesn't mean that you are going to set goals and you are not going to set them aside because other priorities take precedence, as I said earlier, life happens. At the end of the day we had only 24 hours, after that it is simply another day.When people ask me about my goals, and how do I accomplish them, I always reply, that the secret is in the details, all the details and in writing, always in writing.

In May 2011, when I published my first novel, The Writer, the goal on my list said: Publish and begin selling my first novel before the end of 2011. Not only did I publish that novel, I published a second one in December that same year. Both novels reached bestseller status on Smashwords and even with that, at some point in January 2012, I thought that I had failed when my sales slowed down and I didn't know what to do. While I was doing a annual review, I notice that in my goal there was no mention of sales, only publication. My goal was not only accomplished, it had been a success. You can't fail on a goal that doesn't exist. Bu when your goals are in writing, your brain can not convince you that your goal was different. You don't need to win the battle against yourself, when your goals are in writing, is easy to win. In a way, you provide yourself the tools for winning. The interesting thing was that when I set my 2012 goals, I didn't include the numbers, but included other aspects that will allow me to confirm that I tried to sell my books. I can't control if people will buy one book or none, but I can control my effort to sell them or not.

The idea is to define the rules to be able to measure what was accomplished and guarantee that success is possible. The importance of writing your goals down is so you don't forget. When a friend recently opened his office as an independent professional, we spent days writing his goals, in detail. How much money per year, how many working hours every day. How many clients. Things that the office was going to acquire with the profits. A lot of detail; all that we could. When the first month was over (with a positive balance and better than expected), my friend called me. I reminded him to check his list. Immediately, he said that he was going to change some of the goals. And I said, "No." "But with this month's results, maybe I can make double of what I originally planned," he replied. "In that case, you can celebrate that you did double of what you expected in December. But you can't change it, or increase it until you accomplish it, not only the goal but also the time you had established for it. Don't steal from yourself the opportunity to celebrate a victory, to celebrate that you accomplished your goal."

I have stolen many of my own victories, mostly from ignorance. Like my goal of reading 52 books per year. In general, I reach the goal without problems. I have not increased it, not because I can't read more books, but because I love to celebrate the victory.

One of those that I remember was when I learned to type. My goal was 60 words per minute. When I set that goal originally, it seemed impossible. Sixty words per minute were a lot, impossible. The interesting thing is that the first time I reached 60 words per minute, instead of stopping and celebrating, I noticed that 60 words a minute seemed too few. Instead of celebrating, I made out as if it was nothing, something that anyone can do. (I understand that it is true that anyone can type 60 words per minute, but many people don't.) When your goals aren't in writing, you often lose the opportunity of recognizing that you've reached them and enjoying the victory.

We all have more things to do than we can accomplish. We all have fewer hours than what we need. But if we don't mark the precise place where we want to reach, and if we don't establish some place where we want to celebrate, our lives pass without the feeling that we accomplished something. We simply forget what was the goal, and we never get there. We can always do a little more: one more client, one more piece, one more paragraph. There is no problem with that one more paragraph or the one piece more or the extra client; the problem is when you don't celebrate, when you don't celebrate that you reached the point that you thought was worthy of a goal.

Maybe there are two things with this trick, writing and defining your destiny in detail, so once you get there you can make sure you celebrate it, you recognize that you have reach the goal. Don't cheat yourself, don't steal the victories yourself. Stop, celebrate them. Slow down, smile, look where you are now, remember from where you are coming. It is important to celebrate when we accomplish a goal, it's important to remember from where we came. In my experience, with the passage of time, the way to guarantee that we will recognize the place we're going to is when we have described it before we begin the journey, from the place where we were, otherwise it always looks like nothing, and we will try for a little bit more instead of celebrating and then setting a new and bigger goal.

1: THE EXTRAORDINARY HOUR

What would happen if once a week you could stop and forget all your problems, limits, fears, stress, and the things that press on you and focus all your efforts to think? Not just thinking, but thinking about extraordinary things, things worthy of people you admire, things that people you admire would be impressed with, that when you observe your thoughts from the outside, you'd consider them as something just amazing. What if, for sixty minutes, one hour, you concentrated all your efforts on being extraordinary? In doing, creating, and dreaming only on extraordinary things?

The first time that I heard of the "Extraordinary Hour" it was from Michael Bungay Stainer. In his book Do More Great Work, he goes into deep detail about this hour.

Immediately I began to act on his advice and next to my weekly review from Getting things Done, it's been one of my most useful tools. The Extraordinary Hour has allowed me, at least one hour per week, almost every week, to build and dream extraordinary stuff. I am not talking about doing things so people think I am doing my work, or doing good work, this hour is for things that are extraordinary.

For me the Extraordinary Hour is an hour to think. The idea is not to work, I am not looking to solve a specific problem (even though I have solved them) but rather to sit down and think, focus on thinking, (that it is incredibly hard) reaching that place where I leave the noise of the day to day and every day problems behind. The idea of this hour isn't to solve problems that can be defined as good to solve, but problems that when solved will generate incredible results. The difference is simple, all of us can find solutions for those problems that are considered good to solve, but you need to really focus to solve problems that will produce extraordinary results.

There are days when I reach that focused place in ten minutes and other days that takes me fifty (and on some days I can't reach the thinking place at all). The reality is that the time to think is what makes the difference. Some weeks have helped me reinforce things that I have read, others to find solutions to problems and to unstick things that before the Extraordinary Hour, I had no idea how to fix.

For me, this has been an incredible exercise, to sit and write for an hour, as if I was having a conversation with myself. I ask myself questions, I answer those and more. I think on things that can produce incredible results. I allow myself to think on stuff that even I believe is dumb or I am convinced that if people knew about them, they'd declare me irrational or stupid. It's something like an hour for impossibles. It's the weekly permission that I have to think, to stop the race, and try to see things from a different perspective.

Using this trick, I have made million dollar sales, doubled sales, reduced inventory issues, reduced excess inventory, created stories, solved dumb things that have created a positive effect in the way I live my life as well as the life of my family.

One of those things was when I began to handle two big and important accounts for the US e-commerce market. My decision was simple, instead of different prices (what the person that was handling the accounts previously had been doing and the normal practice in the industry), I went to the same pricing for both accounts. I sat with both managers and explained to them that from now on, the cost for both companies was going to be the same. Both threatened to kick me out. After I explained that I was sure that having the same price, we could focus how to grow the market for both companies instead of cents of differences in prices. Both thought that I was crazy. No one had tried that before. The second decision was to reduce inventory based only on current sales and not on projections. Again both thought I was crazy. No one did it that way. Twelve months later, we had doubled sales and reduced the excess inventory by more than 70%. By then I wasn't crazy anymore, and was no longer the irrational person taht I was when I proposed changing the way we were doing things. Both solutions came to me during my Extraordinary Hour. I needed something extraordinary, and that solved my problem that in an ordinary way wasn't going to be solved. These are the kinds of things that I found during my Extraordinary Hour. My hour gives me the chance to slow down, so I can have the luxury to think and I can find the satisfaction of doing something amazing.

The problem that most of us have is that we are going too fast, and we don't stop to think, we think that we don't have time or the luxury to slow down and sit to simply think. In my modest opinion, it's is exactly the opposite; not stopping to think is a luxury that we should not have, without any doubt our world would be a better place if all of us slowed down instead of shooting to see if it works.

Like all the tips in this book, the challenge is simple: try it. Make an appointment in your calendar, one hour. Set an alarm, get a glass of water, and write all that comes to your mind, regardless if it is pending stuff, tasks, dreams, problems, or dumb things. When the good stuff arrives, you will be able to recognize it. Give yourself the chance, the opportunity, or maybe the luxury of having the space to think.

Many times from my hour of thinking I only obtain the satisfaction that I thought for an hour, other times it's even better and I discover things, identify others, or contemplate a future that maybe someday will happen.

One hour a week, simply make it extraordinary; give yourself the chance to slow down, so you have the luxury to think and you'll quickly find the satisfaction of something incredible.

CONCLUSIONS AND LAST NOTES

My love of productivity doesn't make me an expert or a guru. I am simply a human being that during many years has learned that are little tricks that create big results and those are some of the ones that I have presented here. None of these things are big, complex, or costly but the implementation of them (even only one them) can generate good effects and results beyond what you might expect. Many times it's those little things that are the ones that generate the major changes. In addition, it's those little things that we tend to ignore, the ones that we choose to do later.

I am sure there are chapters that will make sense, chapters that you will discover you already do that or some variant, and others that you will skip. The reactions will vary, but these are things that have helped me to be more productive. I believe that many people will skip the chapter on typing, since in general over the yearsI've gotten three kind of reactions to that chapter:

1.- I don't type enough so increasing speed won't have any effect. -- I receive a lot of emails but my answers are short, three lines tops. On average, three lines are 45 words. If your speed is 25 words per minute, you need almost two minutes to reply to each email. If you receive 30 emails, you will lose an hour. Now, learning to type 60 words per minute (that it isn't a big deal, or a reason for a big celebration) you will need only forty five seconds to reply that email. The same 30 emails would take less that twenty three minutes. Repeat that five times a week and you just recovered 185 extra minutes in your life. (That's three extra hours per week!)

2.- I know that increasing my typing speed would give me an advantage, but I don't have the time to learn. -- For some reason, these people ignore that we are talking about five additional hours of freedom to do other activities (five hours that they don't have, and I don't have either) but fifteen minutes Monday to Friday, during your working hours would create an incredible effect. Again, it's those little things that make the big impact.

3.- I type more than X words per minute and I hope next year to type X more. -- This is the smallest group of all. I have found that it is really small the group of people that have recognized the importance of typing and how much that can affect their daily lives.

The 25 tricks in this book weren't discovered by me at once, but without a doubt are things that have helped me to be effective, productive, and to obtain many of my goals.

Like I said at the beginning, I am not a guru nor an expert. I am simply a fan that has discovered that some things, done consistently, generate incredible effects and results.

Thanks for reading this book. I hope that one of these 25 tricks will change your life, or change the life of someone you know. Give it as a gift to someone that you think can benefit from it, they might be grateful to you for the rest of their life.

SPECIAL THANKS

To my wife and my daughter, who are simply amazing. I will never get tired of saying that.

To Tara Rodden Robinson, not only was it a pleasure and honor to have her write the foreword of this book, but she has been a friend, an unconditional supporter, and a teacher.

To Kenn Rudolph, not only my friend but who also created the incredible covers of my books.

To those who always believed in me and who now smile when learning that I am a writer.

To those kind and generous eyes that read this when looked like a minefield, full of spelling and grammar errors.

To my parents, friends and family.

To all those who took the time to read this or any of my books.

To those who had given their reviews on this book or any other of my books.

To those people who in some way or another have helped me make this a reality.

ABOUT THE AUTHOR

Augusto Pinaud currently lives in Fort Wayne, Indiana. He is married and has a little girl and two dogs who keep him company.

He spends his days teaching his daughter, writing, and washing dishes, because he believes in what Agatha Christie once said: "The best time for planning a book is while you're doing the dishes."

My blog: www.augustopinaud.com

Twitter: apinaud

Email: augusto@augustopinaud.com

Facebook: http://www.facebook.com/augustopinaud/

Web Page of the Book:

http://www.25tipsforproductivity.augustopinaud/

Printed in Great Britain
by Amazon.co.uk, Ltd.,
Marston Gate.